Six Short Plays

John Galsworthy

I0136146

Contents

SIX SHORT PLAYS

BY

John Galsworthy

THE FIRST AND THE LAST

A DRAMA IN THREE SCENES

PERSONS OF THE PLAY

KEITH DARRANT, K.C.
LARRY DARRANT, His Brother.
WANDA.

SCENE I. KEITH'S Study.

SCENE II. WANDA's Room.

SCENE III. The Same.

Between SCENE I. and SCENE II.--Thirty hours.
Between SCENE II. and SCENE III.--Two months.

SCENE I

It is six o'clock of a November evening, in KEITH DARRANT'S study. A large, dark-curtained room where the light from a single reading-lamp falling on Turkey carpet, on books beside a large armchair, on the deep blue-and-gold coffee service, makes a sort of oasis before a log fire. In red Turkish slippers and an old brown velvet coat, KEITH DARRANT sits asleep. He has a dark, clean-cut, clean-shaven face, dark grizzling hair, dark twisting eyebrows.

[The curtained door away out in the dim part of the room behind him is opened so softly that he does not wake. LARRY DARRANT enters and stands half lost in the curtain over the door. A thin figure, with a worn, high cheek-boned face, deep-sunk blue eyes and wavy hair all ruffled--a face which still has a certain beauty. He moves inwards along the wall, stands still again and utters a gasping sigh. KEITH stirs in his chair.]

KEITH. Who's there?

LARRY. [In a stifled voice] Only I--Larry.

KEITH. [Half-waked] Come in! I was asleep. [He does not turn his head, staring sleepily at the fire.]

The sound of LARRY's breathing can be heard.

[Turning his head a little] Well, Larry, what is it?

LARRY comes skirting along the wall, as if craving its support, outside the radius of the light.

[Staring] Are you ill?

LARRY stands still again and heaves a deep sigh.

KEITH. [Rising, with his back to the fire, and staring at his brother] What is it, man? [Then with a brutality born of nerves suddenly ruffled] Have you committed a murder that you stand there like a fish?

LARRY. [In a whisper] Yes, Keith.

KEITH. [With vigorous disgust] By Jove! Drunk again! [In a voice changed by sudden apprehension] What do you mean by coming here in this state? I told you---- If you weren't my brother----! Come here, where I can we you! What's the matter with you, Larry?

[With a lurch LARRY leaves the shelter of the wall and sinks into a chair in the circle of light.]

LARRY. It's true.

[KEITH steps quickly forward and stares down into his brother's eyes, where is a horrified wonder, as if they would never again get on terms with his face.]

KEITH. [Angry, bewildered-in a low voice] What in God's name is this nonsense?

[He goes quickly over to the door and draws the curtain aside, to see that it is shut, then comes back to LARRY, who is huddling over the fire.]

Come, Larry! Pull yourself together and drop exaggeration! What on earth do you mean?

LARRY. [In a shrill outburst] It's true, I tell you; I've killed a man.

KEITH. [Bracing himself; coldly] Be quiet!

    LARRY lifts his hands and wrings them.

[Utterly taken aback] Why come here and tell me this?

LARRY. Whom should I tell, Keith? I came to ask what I'm to do--give myself up, or what?

KEITH. When--when--what----?

LARRY. Last night.

KEITH. Good God! How? Where? You'd better tell me quietly from the beginning. Here, drink this coffee; it'll clear your head.

    He pours out and hands him a cup of coffee. LARRY drinks it off.

LARRY. My head! Yes! It's like this, Keith--there's a girl----

KEITH. Women! Always women, with you! Well?

LARRY. A Polish girl. She--her father died over here when she was sixteen, and left her all alone. There was a mongrel living in the same house who married her--or pretended to. She's very pretty, Keith. He left her with a baby coming. She lost it, and nearly starved. Then another fellow took her on, and she lived with him two years, till that brute turned up again and made her go back to him. He used to beat her black and blue. He'd left her again when--I met her. She was taking anybody then. [He stops, passes his hand over his lips, looks up at KEITH, and goes on defiantly] I never met a sweeter woman, or a truer, that I swear. Woman! She's only twenty now! When I went to her last night, that devil had found her out again. He came for me--a bullying, great, hulking brute. Look! [He touches a dark mark on his forehead] I took his ugly throat, and when I let go--[He stops and his hands drop.]

KEITH. Yes?

LARRY. [In a smothered voice] Dead, Keith. I never knew till afterwards that she was hanging on to him--to h-help me. [Again he wrings his hands.]

KEITH. [In a hard, dry voice] What did you do then?

LARRY. We--we sat by it a long time.

KEITH. Well?

LARRY. Then I carried it on my back down the street, round a corner, to an archway.

KEITH. How far?

LARRY. About fifty yards.

KEITH. Was--did anyone see?

LARRY. No.

KEITH. What time?

LARRY. Three in the morning.

KEITH. And then?

LARRY. Went back to her.

KEITH. Why--in heaven's name?

LARRY. She way lonely and afraid. So was I, Keith.

KEITH. Where is this place?

LARRY. Forty-two Borrow Square, Soho.

KEITH. And the archway?

LARRY. Corner of Glove Lane.

KEITH. Good God! Why, I saw it in the paper this morning. They were talking of it in the Courts! [He snatches the evening paper from his armchair, and runs it over anal reads] Here it is again. "Body of a man was found this morning under an archway in Glove Lane. From marks about the throat grave suspicion of foul play are entertained. The body had apparently been robbed." My God! [Suddenly he turns] You saw this in the paper and dreamed it. D'you understand, Larry?--you dreamed it.

LARRY. [Wistfully] If only I had, Keith!

[KEITH makes a movement of his hands almost like his brother's.]

KEITH. Did you take anything from the-body?

LARRY. [Drawing au envelope from his pocket] This dropped out while we were struggling.

KEITH. [Snatching it and reading] "Patrick Walenn"--Was that his name? "Simon's Hotel, Farrier Street, London." [Stooping, he puts it in the fire] No!--that makes me----[He bends to pluck it out, stays his hand, and stamps it suddenly further in with his foot] What in God's name made you come here and tell me? Don't you know I'm--I'm within an ace of a Judgeship?

LARRY. [Simply] Yes. You must know what I ought to do. I didn't, mean to kill him, Keith. I love the girl--I love her. What shall I do?

KEITH. Love!

LARRY. [In a flash] Love!--That swinish brute! A million creatures die every day, and not one of them deserves death as he did. But but I feel it here. [Touching his heart] Such an awful clutch, Keith. Help me if you can, old man. I may be no good, but I've never hurt a fly if I could help it. [He buries his face in his hands.]

KEITH. Steady, Larry! Let's think it out. You weren't seen, you say?

LARRY. It's a dark place, and dead night.

KEITH. When did you leave the girl again?

LARRY. About seven.

KEITH. Where did you go?

LARRY. To my rooms.

KEITH. To Fitzroy Street?

LARRY. Yes.

KEITH. What have you done since?

LARRY. Sat there--thinking.

KEITH. Not been out?

LARRY. No.

KEITH. Not seen the girl?

    [LARRY shakes his head.]

Will she give you away?

LARRY. Never.

KEITH. Or herself hysteria?

LARRY. No.

KEITH. Who knows of your relations with her?

LARRY. No one.

KEITH. No one?

LARRY. I don't know who should, Keith.

KEITH. Did anyone see you go in last night, when you first went to her?

LARRY. No. She lives on the ground floor. I've got keys.

KEITH. Give them to me.

   LARRY takes two keys from his pocket and hands them to his brother.

LARRY. [Rising] I can't be cut off from her!

KEITH. What! A girl like that?

LARRY. [With a flash] Yes, a girl like that.

KEITH. [Moving his hand to put down old emotion] What else have you that connects you with her?

LARRY. Nothing.

KEITH. In your rooms?

   [LARRY shakes his head.]

Photographs? Letters?

LARRY. No.

KEITH. Sure?

LARRY. Nothing.

KEITH. No one saw you going back to her?

[LARRY shakes his head.]
Nor leave in the morning? You can't be certain.

LARRY. I am.

KEITH. You were fortunate. Sit down again, man. I must think.

He turns to the fire and leans his elbows on the mantelpiece and his head on his hands. LARRY Sits down again obediently.

KEITH. It's all too unlikely. It's monstrous!

LARRY. [Sighing it out] Yes.

KEITH. This Walenn--was it his first reappearance after an absence?

LARRY. Yes.

KEITH. How did he find out where she was?

LARRY. I don't know.

KEITH. [Brutally] How drunk were you?

LARRY. I was not drunk.

KEITH. How much had you drunk, then?

LARRY. A little claret--nothing!

KEITH. You say you didn't mean to kill him.

LARRY. God knows.

KEITH. That's something.

LARRY. He hit me. [He holds up his hands] I didn't know I was so strong.

KEITH. She was hanging on to him, you say?--That's ugly.

LARRY. She was scared for me.

KEITH. D'you mean she--loves you?

LARRY. [Simply] Yes, Keith.

KEITH. [Brutally] Can a woman like that love?

LARRY. [Flashing out] By God, you are a stony devil! Why not?

KEITH. [Dryly] I'm trying to get at truth. If you want me to help, I must know everything. What makes you think she's fond of you?

LARRY. [With a crazy laugh] Oh, you lawyer! Were you never in a woman's arms?

KEITH. I'm talking of love.

LARRY. [Fiercely] So am I. I tell you she's devoted. Did you ever pick up a lost dog? Well, she has the lost dog's love for me. And I for her; we picked each other up. I've never felt for another woman what I feel for her--she's been the saving of me!

KEITH. [With a shrug] What made you choose that archway?

LARRY. It was the first dark place.

KEITH. Did his face look as if he'd been strangled?

LARRY. Don't!

KEITH. Did it?

   [LARRY bows his head.]

Very disfigured?

LARRY. Yes.

KEITH. Did you look to see if his clothes were marked?

LARRY. No.

KEITH. Why not?

LARRY. [In an outburst] I'm not made of iron, like you. Why not?
If you had done it----!

KEITH. [Holding up his hand] You say he was disfigured. Would he
be recognisable?

LARRY. [Wearily] I don't know.

KEITH. When she lived with him last--where was that?

LARRY. In Pimlico, I think.

KEITH. Not Soho?

[LARRY shakes his head.]

How long has she been at this Soho place?

LARRY. Nearly a year.

KEITH. Living this life?

LARRY. Till she met me.

KEITH. Till, she met you? And you believe----?

LARRY. [Starting up] Keith!

KEITH. [Again raising his hand] Always in the same rooms?

LARRY. [Subsiding] Yes.

KEITH. What was he? A professional bully?

[LARRY nods.]

Spending most of his time abroad, I suppose.

LARRY. I think so.

KEITH. Can you say if he was known to the police?

LARRY. I've never heard.

KEITH turns away and walks up and down; then, stopping at LARRY's chair, he speaks.

KEITH. Now listen, Larry. When you leave here, go straight home, and stay there till I give you leave to go out again. Promise.

LARRY. I promise.

KEITH. Is your promise worth anything?

LARRY. [With one of his flashes] "Unstable as water, he shall not excel!"

KEITH. Exactly. But if I'm to help you, you must do as I say. I must have time to think this out. Have you got money?

LARRY. Very little.

KEITH. [Grimly] Half-quarter day--yes, your quarter's always spent by then. If you're to get away--never mind, I can manage the money.

LARRY. [Humbly] You're very good, Keith; you've always been very good to me--I don't know why.

KEITH. [Sardonically] Privilege of A brother. As it happens, I'm thinking of myself and our family. You can't indulge yourself in killing without bringing ruin. My God! I suppose you realise that you've made me an accessory after the fact--me, King's counsel--sworn to the service of the Law, who, in a year or two, will have the trying of cases like yours! By heaven, Larry, you've surpassed yourself!

LARRY. [Bringing out a little box] I'd better have done with it.

KErra. You fool! Give that to me.

LARRY. [With a strange smite] No. [He holds up a tabloid between finger and thumb] White magic, Keith! Just one--and they may do what they like to you, and you won't know it. Snap your fingers at all the tortures. It's a great comfort! Have one to keep by you?

KEITH. Come, Larry! Hand it over.

LARRY. [Replacing the box] Not quite! You've never killed a man, you see. [He gives that crazy laugh.] D'you remember that hammer when we were boys and you riled me, up in the long room? I had luck then. I had luck in Naples once. I nearly killed a driver for beating his poor brute of a horse. But now--! My God! [He covers his face.]

    KEITH touched, goes up and lays a hand on his shoulder.

KEITH. Come, Larry! Courage!

    LARRY looks up at him.

LARRY. All right, Keith; I'll try.

KEITH. Don't go out. Don't drink. Don't talk. Pull yourself together!

LARRY. [Moving towards the door] Don't keep me longer than you can help, Keith.

KEITH. No, no. Courage!

    LARRY reaches the door, turns as if to say something-finds no words, and goes.

[To the fire] Courage! My God! I shall need it!

CURTAIN

SCENE II

At out eleven o'clock the following night an WANDA'S room on the
ground floor in Soho. In the light from one close-shaded
electric bulb the room is but dimly visible. A dying fire burns
on the left. A curtained window in the centre of the back wall.
A door on the right. The furniture is plush-covered and
commonplace, with a kind of shabby smartness. A couch, without
back or arms, stands aslant, between window and fire.

[On this WANDA is sitting, her knees drawn up under her, staring
at the embers. She has on only her nightgown and a wrapper over
it; her bare feet are thrust into slippers. Her hands are
crossed and pressed over her breast. She starts and looks up,
listening. Her eyes are candid and startled, her face alabaster
pale, and its pale brown hair, short and square-cut, curls
towards her bare neck. The startled dark eyes and the faint
rose of her lips are like colour-staining on a white mask.]

[Footsteps as of a policeman, very measured, pass on the
pavement outside, and die away. She gets up and steals to the
window, draws one curtain aside so that a chink of the night is

seen. She opens the curtain wider, till the shape of a bare,
witch-like tree becomes visible in the open space of the little
Square on the far side of the road. The footsteps are heard
once more coming nearer. WANDA closes the curtains and cranes
back. They pass and die again. She moves away and looking down
at the floor between door and couch, as though seeing something
there; shudders; covers her eyes; goes back to the couch and
down again just as before, to stare at the embers. Again she is
startled by noise of the outer door being opened. She springs
up, runs and turns the light by a switch close to the door. By
the glimmer of the fire she can just be seen standing by the
dark window-curtains, listening. There comes the sound of
subdued knocking on her door. She stands in breathless terror.
The knocking is repeated. The sound of a latchkey in the door
is heard. Her terror leaves her. The door opens; a man enters
in a dark, fur overcoat.]

WANDA. [In a voice of breathless relief, with a rather foreign
accent] Oh! it's you, Larry! Why did you knock? I was so
frightened. Come in! [She crosses quickly, and flings her arms
round his neck] [Recoiling--in a terror-stricken whisper] Oh! Who
is it?

KEITH. [In a smothered voice] A friend of Larry's. Don't be
frightened.

She has recoiled again to the window; and when he finds the
switch and turns the light up, she is seen standing there
holding her dark wrapper up to her throat, so that her face has
an uncanny look of being detached from the body.

[Gently] You needn't be afraid. I haven't come to do you harm--
quite the contrary. [Holding up the keys] Larry wouldn't have given

me these, would he, if he hadn't trusted me?

> WANDA does not move, staring like a spirit startled out of the flesh.

[After looking round him] I'm sorry to have startled you.

WANDA. [In a whisper] Who are you, please?

KEITH. Larry's brother.

> WANDA, with a sigh of utter relief, steals forward to the couch and sinks down. KEITH goes up to her.

He'd told me.

WANDA. [Clasping her hands round her knees.] Yes?

KEITH. An awful business!

WANDA. Yes; oh, yes! Awful--it is awful!

KEITH. [Staring round him again.] In this room?

WANDA. Just where you are standing. I see him now, always falling.

KEITH. [Moved by the gentle despair in her voice] You--look very young. What's your name?

WANDA. Wanda.

KEITH. Are you fond of Larry?

WANDA. I would die for him!

[A moment's silence.]

KEITH. I--I've come to see what you can do to save him.

WANDA, [Wistfully] You would not deceive me. You are really his brother?

KEITH. I swear it.

WANDA. [Clasping her hands] If I can save him! Won't you sit down?

KEITH. [Drawing up a chair and sitting] This, man, your--your husband, before he came here the night before last--how long since you saw him?

WANDA. Eighteen month.

KEITH. Does anyone about here know you are his wife?

WANDA. No. I came here to live a bad life. Nobody know me. I am quite alone.

KEITH. They've discovered who he was--you know that?

WANDA. No; I have not dared to go out.

KEITH: Well, they have; and they'll look for anyone connected with him, of course.

WANDA. He never let people think I was married to him. I don't know if I was--really. We went to an office and signed our names; but he was a wicked man. He treated many, I think, like me.

KEITH. Did my brother ever see him before?

WANDA. Never! And that man first went for him.

KEITH. Yes. I saw the mark. Have you a servant?

WANDA. No. A woman come at nine in the morning for an hour.

KEITH. Does she know Larry?

WANDA. No. He is always gone.

KEITH. Friends--acquaintances?

WANDA. No; I am verree quiet. Since I know your brother, I see no one, sare.

KEITH. [Sharply] Do you mean that?

WANDA. Oh, yes! I love him. Nobody come here but him for a long time now.

KEITH. How long?

WANDA. Five month.

KEITH. So you have not been out since----?

   [WANDA shakes her head.]

What have you been doing?

WANDA. [Simply] Crying. [Pressing her hands to her breast] He is in danger because of me. I am so afraid for him.

KEITH. [Checking her emotion] Look at me.

[She looks at him.]

If the worst comes, and this man is traced to you, can you trust yourself not to give Larry away?

WANDA. [Rising and pointing to the fire] Look! I have burned all the things he have given me--even his picture. Now I have nothing from him.

KEITH. [Who has risen too] Good! One more question. Do the police know you--because--of your life?

[She looks at him intently, and shakes her, head.]

You know where Larry lives?

WANDA. Yes.

KEITH. You mustn't go there, and he mustn't come to you.

[She bows her head; then, suddenly comes close to him.]

WANDA. Please do not take him from me altogether. I will be so careful. I will not do anything to hurt him. But if I cannot see him sometimes, I shall die. Please do not take him from me.

[She catches his hand and presses it desperately between her own.]

KEITH. Leave that to me. I'm going to do all I can.

WANDA. [Looking up into his face] But you will be kind?

> Suddenly she bends and kisses his hand. KEITH draws his hand
> away, and she recoils a little humbly, looking up at him again.
> Suddenly she stands rigid, listening.

[In a whisper] Listen! Someone--out there!

> She darts past him and turns out the light. There is a knock on
> the door. They are now close together between door and window.

 [Whispering] Oh! Who is it?

KEITH. [Under his breath] You said no one comes but Larry.

WANDA. Yes, and you have his keys. Oh! if it is Larry! I must open!

> KEITH shrinks back against the wall. WANDA goes to the door.

[Opening the door an inch] Yes? Please? Who?

> A thin streak of light from a bull's-eye lantern outside plays
> over the wall. A Policeman's voice says: "All right, Miss.
> Your outer door's open. You ought to keep it shut after dark,
> you know."

WANDA. Thank you, air.

> [The sound of retreating footsteps, of the outer door closing.
> WANDA shuts the door.]

A policeman!

KEITH. [Moving from the wall] Curse! I must have left that door. [Suddenly-turning up the light] You told me they didn't know you.

WANDA. [Sighing] I did not think they did, sir. It is so long I was not out in the town; not since I had Larry.

> KEITH gives her an intent look, then crosses to the fire. He stands there a moment, looking down, then turns to the girl, who has crept back to the couch.

KEITH. [Half to himself] After your life, who can believe---? Look here! You drifted together and you'll drift apart, you know. Better for him to get away and make a clean cut of it.

WANDA. [Uttering a little moaning sound] Oh, sir! May I not love, because I have been bad? I was only sixteen when that man spoiled me. If you knew----

KEITH. I'm thinking of Larry. With you, his danger is much greater. There's a good chance as things are going. You may wreck it. And for what? Just a few months more of--well--you know.

WANDA. [Standing at the head of the couch and touching her eyes with her hands] Oh, sir! Look! It is true. He is my life. Don't take him away from me.

KEITH. [Moved and restless] You must know what Larry is. He'll never stick to you.

WANDA. [Simply] He will, sir.

KEITH. [Energetically] The last man on earth to stick to anything! But for the sake of a whim he'll risk his life and the honour of all his family. I know him.

WANDA. No, no, you do not. It is I who know him.

KEITH. Now, now! At any moment they may find out your connection with that man. So long as Larry goes on with you, he's tied to this murder, don't you see?

WANDA. [Coming close to him] But he love me. Oh, sir! he love me!

KEITH. Larry has loved dozens of women.

WANDA. Yes, but----[Her face quivers].

KEITH. [Brusquely] Don't cry! If I give you money, will you disappear, for his sake?

WANDA. [With a moan] It will be in the water, then. There will be no cruel men there.

KEITH. Ah! First Larry, then you! Come now. It's better for you both. A few months, and you'll forget you ever met.

WANDA. [Looking wildly up] I will go if Larry say I must. But not to live. No! [Simply] I could not, sir.

    [KEITH, moved, is silent.]

I could not live without Larry. What is left for a girl like me-- when she once love? It is finish.

KEITH. I don't want you to go back to that life.

WANDA. No; you do not care what I do. Why should you? I tell you I will go if Larry say I must.

KEITH. That's not enough. You know that. You must take it out of his hands. He will never give up his present for the sake of his future. If you're as fond of him as you say, you'll help to save him.

WANDA. [Below her breath] Yes! Oh, yes! But do not keep him long from me--I beg! [She sinks to the floor and clasps his knees.]

KEITH. Well, well! Get up.

[There is a tap on the window-pane]

Listen!

[A faint, peculiar whistle.]

WANDA. [Springing up] Larry! Oh, thank God!

[She runs to the door, opens it, and goes out to bring him in. KEITH stands waiting, facing the open doorway.]

[LARRY entering with WANDA just behind him.]

LARRY. Keith!

KEITH. [Grimly] So much for your promise not to go out!

LARRY. I've been waiting in for you all day. I couldn't stand it any longer.

KEITH. Exactly!

LARRY. Well, what's the sentence, brother? Transportation for life and then to be fined forty pounds'?

KEITH. So you can joke, can you?

LARRY. Must.

KEITH. A boat leaves for the Argentine the day after to-morrow; you must go by it.

LARRY. [Putting his arms round WANDA, who is standing motionless with her eyes fixed on him] Together, Keith?

KEITH. You can't go together. I'll send her by the next boat.

LARRY. Swear?

KEITH. Yes. You're lucky they're on a false scent.

LARRY. What?

KEITH. You haven't seen it?

LARRY. I've seen nothing, not even a paper.

KEITH. They've taken up a vagabond who robbed the body. He pawned a snake-shaped ring, and they identified this Walenn by it. I've been down and seen him charged myself.

LARRY. With murder?

WANDA. [Faintly] Larry!

KEITH. He's in no danger. They always get the wrong man first.
It'll do him no harm to be locked up a bit--hyena like that. Better
in prison, anyway, than sleeping out under archways in this weather.

LARRY. What was he like, Keith?

KEITH. A little yellow, ragged, lame, unshaven scarecrow of a chap.
They were fools to think he could have had the strength.

LARRY. What! [In an awed voice] Why, I saw him--after I left you
last night.

KEITH. You? Where?

LARRY. By the archway.

KEITH. You went back there?

LARRY. It draws you, Keith.

KErra. You're mad, I think.

LARRY. I talked to him, and he said, "Thank you for this little
chat. It's worth more than money when you're down." Little grey man
like a shaggy animal. And a newspaper boy came up and said: "That's
right, guv'nors! 'Ere's where they found the body--very spot. They
'yn't got 'im yet."

[He laughs; and the terrified girl presses herself against him.]

An innocent man!

KEITH. He's in no danger, I tell you. He could never have strangled----Why, he hadn't the strength of a kitten. Now, Larry! I'll take your berth to-morrow. Here's money [He brings out a pile of notes and puts them on the couch] You can make a new life of it out there together presently, in the sun.

LARRY. [In a whisper] In the sun! "A cup of wine and thou." [Suddenly] How can I, Keith? I must see how it goes with that poor devil.

KEITH. Bosh! Dismiss it from your mind; there's not nearly enough evidence.

LARRY. Not?

KEITH. No. You've got your chance. Take it like a man.

LARRY. [With a strange smile--to the girl] Shall we, Wanda?

WANDA. Oh, Larry!

LARRY. [Picking the notes up from the couch] Take them back, Keith.

KEITH. What! I tell you no jury would convict; and if they did, no judge would hang. A ghoul who can rob a dead body, ought to be in prison. He did worse than you.

LARRY. It won't do, Keith. I must see it out.

KEITH. Don't be a fool!

LARRY. I've still got some kind of honour. If I clear out before I know, I shall have none--nor peace. Take them, Keith, or I'll put them in the fire.

KEITH. [Taking back the notes; bitterly] I suppose I may ask you not to be entirely oblivious of our name. Or is that unworthy of your honour?

LARRY. [Hanging his head] I'm awfully sorry, Keith; awfully sorry, old man.

KEITH. [sternly] You owe it to me--to our name--to our dead mother --to do nothing anyway till we see what happens.

LARRY. I know. I'll do nothing without you, Keith.

KEITH. [Taking up his hat] Can I trust you? [He stares hard at his brother.]

LARRY. You can trust me.

KEITH. Swear?

LARRY. I swear.

KEITH. Remember, nothing! Good night!

LARRY. Good night!

    KEITH goes. LARRY Sits down on the couch sand stares at the fire. The girl steals up and slips her arms about him.

LARRY. An innocent man!

WANDA. Oh, Larry! But so are you. What did we want--to kill that man? Never! Oh! kiss me!

[LARRY turns his face. She kisses his lips.]

I have suffered so--not seein' you. Don't leave me again--don't! Stay here. Isn't it good to be together?--Oh! Poor Larry! How tired you look!--Stay with me. I am so frightened all alone. So frightened they will take you from me.

LARRY. Poor child!

WANDA. No, no! Don't look like that!

LARRY. You're shivering.

WANDA. I will make up the fire. Love me, Larry! I want to forget.

LARRY. The poorest little wretch on God's earth--locked up--for me! A little wild animal, locked up. There he goes, up and down, up and down--in his cage--don't you see him?--looking for a place to gnaw his way through--little grey rat. [He gets up and roams about.]

WANDA. No, no! I can't bear it! Don't frighten me more!

[He comes back and takes her in his arms.]

LARRY. There, there! [He kisses her closed eyes.]

WANDA. [Without moving] If we could sleep a little--wouldn't it be nice?

LARRY. Sleep?

WANDA. [Raising herself] Promise to stay with me--to stay here for good, Larry. I will cook for you; I will make you so comfortable. They will find him innocent. And then--Oh, Larry! in the sun-right away--far from this horrible country. How lovely! [Trying to get him to look at her] Larry!

LARRY. [With a movement to free 'himself] To the edge of the world-and---over!

WANDA. No, no! No, no! You don't want me to die, Larry, do you? I shall if you leave me. Let us be happy! Love me!

LARRY. [With a laugh] Ah! Let's be happy and shut out the sight of him. Who cares? Millions suffer for no mortal reason. Let's be strong, like Keith. No! I won't leave you, Wanda. Let's forget everything except ourselves. [Suddenly] There he goes-up and down!

WANDA. [Moaning] No, no! See! I will pray to the Virgin. She will pity us!

She falls on her knees and clasps her hands, praying. Her lips move. LARRY stands motionless, with arms crossed, and on his face are yearning and mockery, love and despair.

LARRY. [Whispering] Pray for us! Bravo! Pray away!

[Suddenly the girl stretches out her arms and lifts her face with a look of ecstasy.]

What?

WANDA. She is smiling! We shall be happy soon.

LARRY. [Bending down over her] Poor child! When we die, Wanda, let's go together. We should keep each other warm out in the dark.

WANDA. [Raising her hands to his face] Yes! oh, yes! If you die I could not--I could not go on living!

CURTAIN

SCENE III.

TWO MONTHS LATER

WANDA'S room. Daylight is just beginning to fail of a January afternoon. The table is laid for supper, with decanters of wine.

WANDA is standing at the window looking out at the wintry trees of the Square beyond the pavement. A newspaper Boy's voice is heard coming nearer.

VOICE. Pyper! Glove Lyne murder! Trial and verdict! [Receding] Verdict! Pyper!

WANDA throws up the window as if to call to him, checks herself, closes it and runs to the door. She opens it, but recoils into the room. KEITH is standing there. He comes in.

KEITH. Where's Larry?

WANDA. He went to the trial. I could not keep him from it. The trial--Oh! what has happened, sir?

KEITH. [Savagely] Guilty! Sentence of death! Fools!--idiots!

WANDA. Of death! [For a moment she seems about to swoon.]

KEITH. Girl! girl! It may all depend on you. Larry's still living here?

WANDA. Yes.

KEITH. I must wait for him.

WANDA. Will you sit down, please?

KEITH. [Shaking his head] Are you ready to go away at any time?

WANDA. Yes, yes; always I am ready.

KEITH. And he?

WANDA. Yes--but now! What will he do? That poor man!

KEITH. A graveyard thief--a ghoul!

WANDA. Perhaps he was hungry. I have been hungry: you do things then that you would not. Larry has thought of him in prison so much all these weeks. Oh! what shall we do now?

KEITH. Listen! Help me. Don't let Larry out of your sight. I must see how things go. They'll never hang this wretch. [He grips her arms] Now, we must stop Larry from giving himself up. He's fool enough. D'you understand?

WANDA. Yes. But why has he not come in? Oh! If he have, already!

KEITH. [Letting go her arms] My God! If the police come--find me here--[He moves to the door] No, he wouldn't without seeing you first. He's sure to come. Watch him like a lynx. Don't let him go without you.

WANDA. [Clasping her hands on her breast] I will try, sir.

KEITH. Listen!

[A key is heard in the lock.]

It's he!

LARRY enters. He is holding a great bunch of pink lilies and white narcissus. His face tells nothing. KEITH looks from him to the girl, who stands motionless.

LARRY. Keith! So you've seen?

KEITH. The thing can't stand. I'll stop it somehow. But you must give me time, Larry.

LARRY. [Calmly] Still looking after your honour, KEITH!

KEITH. [Grimly] Think my reasons what you like.

WANDA. [Softly] Larry!

[LARRY puts his arm round her.]

LARRY. Sorry, old man.

KEITH. This man can and shall get off. I want your solemn promise that you won't give yourself up, nor even go out till I've seen you again.

LARRY. I give it.

KEITH. [Looking from one to the other] By the memory of our mother, swear that.

LARRY. [With a smile] I swear.

KEITH. I have your oath--both of you--both of you. I'm going at once to see what can be done.

LARRY. [Softly] Good luck, brother.

   KEITH goes out.

WANDA. [Putting her hands on LARRY's breast] What does it mean?

LARRY. Supper, child--I've had nothing all day. Put these lilies in water.

   [She takes the lilies and obediently puts them into a vase.
   LARRY pours wine into a deep-coloured glass and drinks it off.]

We've had a good time, Wanda. Best time I ever had, these last two months; and nothing but the bill to pay.

WANDA. [Clasping him desperately] Oh, Larry! Larry!

LARRY. [Holding her away to look at her.] Take off those things and
put on a bridal garment.

WANDA. Promise me--wherever you go, I go too. Promise! Larry, you
think I haven't seen, all these weeks. But I have seen everything;
all in your heart, always. You cannot hide from me. I knew--I knew!
Oh, if we might go away into the sun! Oh! Larry--couldn't we? [She
searches his eyes with hers--then shuddering] Well! If it must be
dark--I don't care, if I may go in your arms. In prison we could not
be together. I am ready. Only love me first. Don't let me cry
before I go. Oh! Larry, will there be much pain?

LARRY. [In a choked voice] No pain, my pretty.

WANDA. [With a little sigh] It is a pity.

LARRY. If you had seen him, as I have, all day, being tortured.
Wanda,--we shall be out of it. [The wine mounting to his head] We
shall be free in the dark; free of their cursed inhumanities. I hate
this world--I loathe it! I hate its God-forsaken savagery; its pride
and smugness! Keith's world--all righteous will-power and success.
We're no good here, you and I--we were cast out at birth--soft,
will-less--better dead. No fear, Keith! I'm staying indoors. [He
pours wine into two glasses] Drink it up!

    [Obediently WANDA drinks, and he also.]

Now go and make yourself beautiful.

WANDA. [Seizing him in her arms] Oh, Larry!

LARRY. [Touching her face and hair] Hanged by the neck until he's dead--for what I did.

[WANDA takes a long look at his face, slips her arms from him, and goes out through the curtains below the fireplace.]

[LARRY feels in his pocket, brings out the little box, opens it, fingers the white tabloids.]

LARRY. Two each--after food. [He laughs and puts back the box] Oh! my girl!

[The sound of a piano playing a faint festive tune is heard afar off. He mutters, staring at the fire.]

[Flames-flame, and flicker-ashes.]

"No more, no more, the moon is dead, And all the people in it."

[He sits on the couch with a piece of paper on his knees, adding a few words with a stylo pen to what is already written.]

[The GIRL, in a silk wrapper, coming back through the curtains, watches him.]

LARRY. [Looking up] It's all here--I've confessed. [Reading]

"Please bury us together."
"LAURENCE DARRANT.
"January 28th, about six p.m."

They'll find us in the morning. Come and have supper, my dear love.

[The girl creeps forward. He rises, puts his arm round her, and with her arm twined round him, smiling into each other's faces, they go to the table and sit down.]

The curtain falls for a few seconds to indicate the passage of three hours. When it rises again, the lovers are lying on the couch, in each other's arms, the lilies stream about them. The girl's bare arm is round LARRY'S neck. Her eyes are closed; his are open and sightless. There is no light but fire-light.

A knocking on the door and the sound of a key turned in the lock. KEITH enters. He stands a moment bewildered by the half-light, then calls sharply: "Larry!" and turns up the light. Seeing the forms on the couch, he recoils a moment. Then, glancing at the table and empty decanters, goes up to the couch.

KEITH. [Muttering] Asleep! Drunk! Ugh!

[Suddenly he bends, touches LARRY, and springs back.]

What! [He bends again, shakes him and calls] Larry! Larry!

[Then, motionless, he stares down at his brother's open, sightless eyes. Suddenly he wets his finger and holds it to the girl's lips, then to LARRY'S.]

[He bends and listens at their hearts; catches sight of the little box lying between them and takes it up.]

My God!

[Then, raising himself, he closes his brother's eyes, and as he does so, catches sight of a paper pinned to the couch; detaches it and reads:]

"I, Lawrence Darrant, about to die by my own hand confess that I----"

[He reads on silently, in horror; finishes, letting the paper drop, and recoils from the couch on to a chair at the dishevelled supper table. Aghast, he sits there. Suddenly he mutters:]

If I leave that there--my name--my whole future!

[He springs up, takes up the paper again, and again reads.]

My God! It's ruin!

[He makes as if to tear it across, stops, and looks down at those two; covers his eyes with his hand; drops the paper and rushes to the door. But he stops there and comes back, magnetised, as it were, by that paper. He takes it up once more and thrusts it into his pocket.]

[The footsteps of a Policeman pass, slow and regular, outside. His face crisps and quivers; he stands listening till they die away. Then he snatches the paper from his pocket, and goes past the foot of the couch to the fore.]

All my----No! Let him hang!

[He thrusts the paper into the fire, stamps it down with his foot, watches it writhe and blacken. Then suddenly clutching his head, he turns to the bodies on the couch. Panting and like a man demented, he recoils past the head of the couch, and rushing to the window, draws the curtains and throws the window up for air. Out in the darkness rises the witch-like skeleton tree, where a dark shape seems hanging. KEITH starts back.]

What's that? What----!

[He shuts the window and draws the dark curtains across it
again.]

Fool! Nothing!

[Clenching his fists, he draws himself up, steadying himself
with all his might. Then slowly he moves to the door, stands a
second like a carved figure, his face hard as stone.]

[Deliberately he turns out the light, opens the door, and goes.]

[The still bodies lie there before the fire which is licking at
the last blackened wafer.]

CURTAIN

THE LITTLE MAN

A FARCICAL MORALITY IN THREE SCENES

CHARACTERS

THE LITTLE MAN.
THE AMERICAN.
THE ENGLISHMAN.
THE ENGLISHWOMAN.
THE GERMAN.
THE DUTCH BOY.
THE MOTHER.
THE BABY.
THE WAITER.
THE STATION OFFICIAL.
THE POLICEMAN.
THE PORTER.

SCENE I

Afternoon, on the departure platform of an Austrian railway
station. At several little tables outside the buffet persons
are taking refreshment, served by a pale young waiter. On a
seat against the wall of the buffet a woman of lowly station is
sitting beside two large bundles, on one of which she has placed
her baby, swathed in a black shawl.

WAITER. [Approaching a table whereat sit an English traveller and
his wife] Two coffee?

ENGLISHMAN. [Paying] Thanks. [To his wife, in an Oxford voice]
Sugar?

ENGLISHWOMAN. [In a Cambridge voice] One.

AMERICAN TRAVELLER. [With field-glasses and a pocket camera from
another table] Waiter, I'd like to have you get my eggs. I've been
sitting here quite a while.

WAITER. Yes, sare.

GERMAN TRAVELLER. 'Kellner, bezahlen'! [His voice is, like his
moustache, stiff and brushed up at the ends. His figure also is
stiff and his hair a little grey; clearly once, if not now, a
colonel.]

WAITER. 'Komm' gleich'!

[The baby on the bundle wails. The mother takes it up to soothe
it. A young, red-cheeked Dutchman at the fourth table stops

eating and laughs.]

AMERICAN. My eggs! Get a wiggle on you!

WAITER. Yes, sare. [He rapidly recedes.]

[A LITTLE MAN in a soft hat is seen to the right of tables. He stands a moment looking after the hurrying waiter, then seats himself at the fifth table.]

ENGLISHMAN. [Looking at his watch] Ten minutes more.

ENGLISHWOMAN. Bother!

AMERICAN. [Addressing them] 'Pears as if they'd a prejudice against eggs here, anyway.

[The ENGLISH look at him, but do not speak.]

GERMAN. [In creditable English] In these places man can get nothing.

[The WAITER comes flying back with a compote for the DUTCH YOUTH, who pays.]

GERMAN. 'Kellner, bezahlen'!

WAITER. 'Eine Krone sechzig'.

[The GERMAN pays.]

AMERICAN. [Rising, and taking out his watch--blandly] See here. If I don't get my eggs before this watch ticks twenty, there'll be another waiter in heaven.

WAITER. [Flying] 'Komm' gleich'!

AMERICAN. [Seeking sympathy] I'm gettin' kind of mad!

[The ENGLISHMAN halves his newspaper and hands the advertisement half to his wife. The BABY wails. The MOTHER rocks it.]

[The DUTCH YOUTH stops eating and laughs. The GERMAN lights a cigarette. The LITTLE MAN sits motionless, nursing his hat. The WAITER comes flying back with the eggs and places them before the AMERICAN.]

AMERICAN. [Putting away his watch] Good! I don't like trouble. How much?

[He pays and eats. The WAITER stands a moment at the edge of the platform and passes his hand across his brow. The LITTLE MAN eyes him and speaks gently.]

LITTLE MAN. Herr Ober!

[The WAITER turns.]

Might I have a glass of beer?

WAITER. Yes, sare.

LITTLE MAN. Thank you very much.

[The WAITER goes.]

AMERICAN. [Pausing in the deglutition of his eggs--affably] Pardon me, sir; I'd like to have you tell me why you called that little bit of a feller "Herr Ober." Reckon you would know what that means? Mr. Head Waiter.

LITTLE MAN. Yes, yes.

AMERICAN. I smile.

LITTLE MAN. Oughtn't I to call him that?

GERMAN. [Abruptly] 'Nein--Kellner'.

AMERICAN. Why, yes! Just "waiter."

[The ENGLISHWOMAN looks round her paper for a second. The DUTCH YOUTH stops eating and laughs. The LITTLE MAN gazes from face to face and nurses his hat.]

LITTLE MAN. I didn't want to hurt his feelings.

GERMAN. Gott!

AMERICAN. In my country we're very democratic--but that's quite a proposition.

ENGLISHMAN. [Handling coffee-pot, to his wife] More?

ENGLISHWOMAN. No, thanks.

GERMAN. [Abruptly] These fellows--if you treat them in this manner, at once they take liberties. You see, you will not get your beer.

[As he speaks the WAITER returns, bringing the LITTLE MAN'S beer, then retires.]

AMERICAN. That 'pears to be one up to democracy. [To the LITTLE MAN] I judge you go in for brotherhood?

LITTLE MAN. [Startled] Oh, no!

AMERICAN. I take considerable stock in Leo Tolstoi myself. Grand man--grand-souled apparatus. But I guess you've got to pinch those waiters some to make 'em skip. [To the ENGLISH, who have carelessly looked his way for a moment] You'll appreciate that, the way he acted about my eggs.

  [The ENGLISH make faint motions with their chins and avert their eyes.]

  [To the WAITER, who is standing at the door of the buffet]

Waiter! Flash of beer--jump, now!

WAITER. 'Komm' gleich'!

GERMAN. 'Cigarren'!

WAITER. 'Schon'!

  [He disappears.]

AMERICAN. [Affably--to the LITTLE MAN] Now, if I don't get that flash of beer quicker'n you got yours, I shall admire.

GERMAN. [Abruptly] Tolstoi is nothing 'nichts'! No good! Ha?

AMERICAN. [Relishing the approach of argument] Well, that is a matter of temperament. Now, I'm all for equality. See that poor woman there--very humble woman--there she sits among us with her baby. Perhaps you'd like to locate her somewhere else?

GERMAN. [Shrugging]. Tolstoi is 'sentimentalisch'. Nietzsche is the true philosopher, the only one.

AMERICAN. Well, that's quite in the prospectus--very stimulating party--old Nietch--virgin mind. But give me Leo! [He turns to the red-cheeked YOUTH] What do you opine, sir? I guess by your labels you'll be Dutch. Do they read Tolstoi in your country?

[The DUTCH YOUTH laughs.]

AMERICAN. That is a very luminous answer.

GERMAN. Tolstoi is nothing. Man should himself express. He must push--he must be strong.

AMERICAN. That is so. In America we believe in virility; we like a man to expand. But we believe in brotherhood too. We draw the line at niggers; but we aspire. Social barriers and distinctions we've not much use for.

ENGLISHMAN. Do you feel a draught?

ENGLISHWOMAN. [With a shiver of her shoulder toward the AMERICAN] I
do--rather.

GERMAN. Wait! You are a young people.

AMERICAN. That is so; there are no flies on us. [To the LITTLE MAN, who has been gazing eagerly from face to face] Say! I'd like to have you give us your sentiments in relation to the duty of man.

[The LITTLE MAN, fidgets, and is about to opens his mouth.]

AMERICAN. For example--is it your opinion that we should kill off the weak and diseased, and all that can't jump around?

GERMAN. [Nodding] 'Ja, ja'! That is coming.

LITTLE MAN. [Looking from face to face] They might be me.

[The DUTCH YOUTH laughs.]

AMERICAN. [Reproving him with a look] That's true humility. 'Tisn't grammar. Now, here's a proposition that brings it nearer the bone: Would you step out of your way to help them when it was liable to bring you trouble?

GERMAN. 'Nein, nein'! That is stupid.

LITTLE MAN. [Eager but wistful] I'm afraid not. Of course one wants to--There was St Francis d'Assisi and St Julien L'Hospitalier, and----

AMERICAN. Very lofty dispositions. Guess they died of them. [He rises] Shake hands, sir--my name is--[He hands a card] I am an ice-machine maker. [He shakes the LITTLE MAN's hand] I like your sentiments--I feel kind of brotherly. [Catching sight of the WAITER appearing in the doorway] Waiter; where to h-ll is that glass of beer?

GERMAN. Cigarren!

WAITER. 'Komm' gleich'!

ENGLISHMAN. [Consulting watch] Train's late.

ENGLISHWOMAN. Really! Nuisance!

[A station POLICEMAN, very square and uniformed, passes and repasses.]

AMERICAN. [Resuming his seat--to the GERMAN] Now, we don't have so much of that in America. Guess we feel more to trust in human nature.

GERMAN. Ah! ha! you will bresently find there is nothing in him but self.

LITTLE MAN. [Wistfully] Don't you believe in human nature?

AMERICAN. Very stimulating question.

[He looks round for opinions. The DUTCH YOUTH laughs.]

ENGLISHMAN. [Holding out his half of the paper to his wife] Swap!

[His wife swaps.]

GERMAN. In human nature I believe so far as I can see him--no more.

AMERICAN. Now that 'pears to me kind o' blasphemy. I believe in heroism. I opine there's not one of us settin' around here that's not a hero--give him the occasion.

LITTLE MAN. Oh! Do you believe that?

AMERICAN. Well! I judge a hero is just a person that'll help another at the expense of himself. Take that poor woman there. Well, now, she's a heroine, I guess. She would die for her baby any old time.

GERMAN. Animals will die for their babies. That is nothing.

AMERICAN. I carry it further. I postulate we would all die for that baby if a locomotive was to trundle up right here and try to handle it. [To the GERMAN] I guess you don't know how good you are. [As the GERMAN is twisting up the ends of his moustache--to the ENGLISHWOMAN] I should like to have you express an opinion, ma'am.

ENGLISHWOMAN. I beg your pardon.

AMERICAN. The English are very humanitarian; they have a very high sense of duty. So have the Germans, so have the Americans. [To the DUTCH YOUTH] I judge even in your little country they have that. This is an epoch of equality and high-toned ideals. [To the LITTLE MAN] What is your nationality, sir?

LITTLE MAN. I'm afraid I'm nothing particular. My father was half-English and half-American, and my mother half-German and half-Dutch.

AMERICAN. My! That's a bit streaky, any old way. [The POLICEMAN passes again] Now, I don't believe we've much use any more for those gentlemen in buttons. We've grown kind of mild--we don't think of self as we used to do.

[The WAITER has appeared in the doorway.]

GERMAN. [In a voice of thunder] 'Cigarren! Donnerwetter'!

AMERICAN. [Shaking his fist at the vanishing WAITER] That flash of beer!

WAITER. 'Komm' gleich'!

AMERICAN. A little more, and he will join George Washington! I was about to remark when he intruded: In this year of grace 1913 the kingdom of Christ is quite a going concern. We are mighty near universal brotherhood. The colonel here [He indicates the GERMAN] is a man of blood and iron, but give him an opportunity to be magnanimous, and he'll be right there. Oh, sir! yep!

  [The GERMAN, with a profound mixture of pleasure and cynicism, brushes up the ends of his moustache.]

LITTLE MAN. I wonder. One wants to, but somehow--[He shakes his head.]

AMERICAN. You seem kind of skeery about that. You've had experience, maybe. I'm an optimist--I think we're bound to make the devil hum in the near future. I opine we shall occasion a good deal of trouble to that old party. There's about to be a holocaust of selfish interests. The colonel there with old-man Nietch he won't know himself. There's going to be a very sacred opportunity.

  [As he speaks, the voice of a RAILWAY OFFICIAL is heard an the distance calling out in German. It approaches, and the words become audible.]

GERMAN. [Startled] 'Der Teufel'! [He gets up, and seizes the bag beside him.]

[The STATION OFFICIAL has appeared; he stands for a moment
casting his commands at the seated group. The DUTCH YOUTH also
rises, and takes his coat and hat. The OFFICIAL turns on his
heel and retires still issuing directions.]

ENGLISHMAN. What does he say?

GERMAN. Our drain has come in, de oder platform; only one minute we
haf.

[All, have risen in a fluster.]

AMERICAN. Now, that's very provoking. I won't get that flash of
beer.

[There is a general scurry to gather coats and hats and wraps,
during which the lowly WOMAN is seen making desperate attempts
to deal with her baby and the two large bundles. Quite
defeated, she suddenly puts all down, wrings her hands, and
cries out: "Herr Jesu! Hilfe!" The flying procession turn
their heads at that strange cry.]

AMERICAN. What's that? Help?

[He continues to run. The LITTLE MAN spins round, rushes back,
picks up baby and bundle on which it was seated.]

LITTLE MAN. Come along, good woman, come along!

[The WOMAN picks up the other bundle and they run.]

[The WAITER, appearing in the doorway with the bottle of beer, watches with his tired smile.]

CURTAIN

SCENE II

A second-class compartment of a corridor carriage, in motion.
In it are seated the ENGLISHMAN and his WIFE, opposite each
other at the corridor end, she with her face to the engine, he
with his back. Both are somewhat protected from the rest of the
travellers by newspapers. Next to her sits the GERMAN, and
opposite him sits the AMERICAN; next the AMERICAN in one window
corner is seated the DUTCH YOUTH; the other window corner is
taken by the GERMAN'S bag. The silence is only broken by the
slight rushing noise of the train's progression and the
crackling of the English newspapers.

AMERICAN. [Turning to the DUTCH YOUTH] Guess I'd like that window raised; it's kind of chilly after that old run they gave us.

[The DUTCH YOUTH laughs, and goes through the motions of raising
the window. The ENGLISH regard the operation with uneasy
irritation. The GERMAN opens his bag, which reposes on the
corner seat next him, and takes out a book.]

AMERICAN. The Germans are great readers. Very stimulating practice. I read most anything myself!

[The GERMAN holds up the book so that the title may be read.]

"Don Quixote"--fine book. We Americans take considerable stock in old man Quixote. Bit of a wild-cat--but we don't laugh at him.

GERMAN. He is dead. Dead as a sheep. A good thing, too.

AMERICAN. In America we have still quite an amount of chivalry.

GERMAN. Chivalry is nothing 'sentimentalisch'. In modern days--no good. A man must push, he must pull.

AMERICAN. So you say. But I judge your form of chivalry is sacrifice to the state. We allow more freedom to the individual soul. Where there's something little and weak, we feel it kind of noble to give up to it. That way we feel elevated.

   [As he speaks there is seen in the corridor doorway the LITTLE
   MAN, with the WOMAN'S BABY still on his arm and the bundle held
   in the other hand. He peers in anxiously. The ENGLISH, acutely
   conscious, try to dissociate themselves from his presence with
   their papers. The DUTCH YOUTH laughs.]

GERMAN. 'Ach'! So!

AMERICAN. Dear me!

LITTLE MAN. Is there room? I can't find a seat.

AMERICAN. Why, yes! There's a seat for one.

LITTLE MAN. [Depositing bundle outside, and heaving BABY] May I?

AMERICAN. Come right in!

[The GERMAN sulkily moves his bag. The LITTLE MAN comes in and seats himself gingerly.]

AMERICAN. Where's the mother?

LITTLE MAN. [Ruefully] Afraid she got left behind.

[The DUTCH YOUTH laughs. The ENGLISH unconsciously emerge from their newspapers.]

AMERICAN. My! That would appear to be quite a domestic incident.

[The ENGLISHMAN suddenly utters a profound "Ha, Ha!" and disappears behind his paper. And that paper and the one opposite are seen to shake, and little sguirls and squeaks emerge.]

GERMAN. And you haf got her bundle, and her baby. Ha! [He cackles drily.]

AMERICAN. [Gravely] I smile. I guess Providence has played it pretty low down on you. It's sure acted real mean.

[The BABY wails, and the LITTLE MAN jigs it with a sort of gentle desperation, looking apologetically from face to face. His wistful glance renews the fore of merriment wherever it alights. The AMERICAN alone preserves a gravity which seems incapable of being broken.]

AMERICAN. Maybe you'd better get off right smart and restore that baby. There's nothing can act madder than a mother.

LITTLE MAN. Poor thing, yes! What she must be suffering!

[A gale of laughter shakes the carriage. The ENGLISH for a
moment drop their papers, the better to indulge. The LITTLE MAN
smiles a wintry smile.]

AMERICAN. [In a lull] How did it eventuate?

LITTLE MAN. We got there just as the train was going to start; and I
jumped, thinking I could help her up. But it moved too quickly,
and--and left her.

[The gale of laughter blows up again.]

AMERICAN. Guess I'd have thrown the baby out to her.

LITTLE MAN. I was afraid the poor little thing might break.

[The Baby wails; the LITTLE MAN heaves it; the gale of laughter
blows.]

AMERICAN. [Gravely] It's highly entertaining--not for the baby.
What kind of an old baby is it, anyway? [He sniff's] I judge it's a
bit--niffy.

LITTLE MAN. Afraid I've hardly looked at it yet.

AMERICAN. Which end up is it?

LITTLE MAM. Oh! I think the right end. Yes, yes, it is.

AMERICAN. Well, that's something. Maybe you should hold it out of
window a bit. Very excitable things, babies!

ENGLISHWOMAN. [Galvanized] No, no!

ENGLISHMAN. [Touching her knee] My dear!

AMERICAN. You are right, ma'am. I opine there's a draught out there. This baby is precious. We've all of us got stock in this baby in a manner of speaking. This is a little bit of universal brotherhood. Is it a woman baby?

LITTLE MAN. I--I can only see the top of its head.

AMERICAN. You can't always tell from that. It looks kind of over-wrapped up. Maybe it had better be unbound.

GERMAN. 'Nein, nein, nein'!

AMERICAN. I think you are very likely right, colonel. It might be a pity to unbind that baby. I guess the lady should be consulted in this matter.

ENGLISHWOMAN. Yes, yes, of course----!

ENGLISHMAN. [Touching her] Let it be! Little beggar seems all right.

AMERICAN. That would seem only known to Providence at this moment. I judge it might be due to humanity to look at its face.

LITTLE MAN. [Gladly] It's sucking my' finger. There, there--nice little thing--there!

AMERICAN. I would surmise in your leisure moments you have created babies, sir?

LITTLE MAN. Oh! no--indeed, no.

AMERICAN. Dear me!--That is a loss. [Addressing himself to the carriage at large] I think we may esteem ourselves fortunate to have this little stranger right here with us. Demonstrates what a hold the little and weak have upon us nowadays. The colonel here--a man of blood and iron--there he sits quite calm next door to it. [He sniffs] Now, this baby is rather chastening--that is a sign of grace, in the colonel--that is true heroism.

LITTLE MAN. [Faintly] I--I can see its face a little now.

   [All bend forward.]

AMERICAN. What sort of a physiognomy has it, anyway?

LITTLE MAN. [Still faintly] I don't see anything but--but spots.

GERMAN. Oh! Ha! Pfui!

   [The DUTCH YOUTH laughs.]

AMERICAN. I am told that is not uncommon amongst babies. Perhaps we could have you inform us, ma'am.

ENGLISHWOMAN. Yes, of course--only what sort of----

LITTLE MAN. They seem all over its----[At the slight recoil of everyone] I feel sure it's--it's quite a good baby underneath.

AMERICAN. That will be rather difficult to come at. I'm just a bit sensitive. I've very little use for affections of the epidermis.

GERMAN. Pfui! [He has edged away as far as he can get, and is lighting a big cigar]

[The DUTCH YOUTH draws his legs back.]

AMERICAN. [Also taking out a cigar] I guess it would be well to fumigate this carriage. Does it suffer, do you think?

LITTLE MAN. [Peering] Really, I don't--I'm not sure--I know so little about babies. I think it would have a nice expression--if--if it showed.

AMERICAN. Is it kind of boiled looking?

LITTLE MAN. Yes--yes, it is.

AMERICAN. [Looking gravely round] I judge this baby has the measles.

[The GERMAN screws himself spasmodically against the arm of the ENGLISHWOMAN'S seat.]

ENGLISHWOMAN. Poor little thing! Shall I----?

[She half rises.]

ENGLISHMAN. [Touching her] No, no----Dash it!

AMERICAN. I honour your emotion, ma'am. It does credit to us all. But I sympathize with your husband too. The measles is a very important pestilence in connection with a grown woman.

LITTLE MAN. It likes my finger awfully. Really, it's rather a sweet baby.

AMERICAN. [Sniffing] Well, that would appear to be quite a question. About them spots, now? Are they rosy?

LITTLE MAN. No-o; they're dark, almost black.

GERMAN. Gott! Typhus! [He bounds up on to the arm of the ENGLISHWOMAN'S Seat.]

AMERICAN. Typhus! That's quite an indisposition!

[The DUTCH YOUTH rises suddenly, and bolts out into the corridor. He is followed by the GERMAN, puffing clouds of smoke. The ENGLISH and AMERICAN sit a moment longer without speaking. The ENGLISHWOMAN'S face is turned with a curious expression--half pity, half fear--towards the LITTLE MAN. Then the ENGLISHMAN gets up.]

ENGLISHMAN. Bit stuffy for you here, dear, isn't it?

[He puts his arm through hers, raises her, and almost pushes her through the doorway. She goes, still looking back.]

AMERICAN. [Gravely] There's nothing I admire more'n courage. Guess I'll go and smoke in the corridor.

[As he goes out the LITTLE MAN looks very wistfully after him. Screwing up his mouth and nose, he holds the BABY away from him and wavers; then rising, he puts it on the seat opposite and goes through the motions of letting down the window. Having done so he looks at the BABY, who has begun to wail. Suddenly he raises his hands and clasps them, like a child praying.

Since, however, the BABY does not stop wailing, he hovers over it in indecision; then, picking it up, sits down again to dandle it, with his face turned toward the open window. Finding that it still wails, he begins to sing to it in a cracked little voice. It is charmed at once. While he is singing, the AMERICAN appears in the corridor. Letting down the passage window, he stands there in the doorway with the draught blowing his hair and the smoke of his cigar all about him. The LITTLE MAN stops singing and shifts the shawl higher to protect the BABY'S head from the draught.]

AMERICAN. [Gravely] This is the most sublime spectacle I have ever envisaged. There ought to be a record of this.

[The LITTLE MAN looks at him, wondering. You are typical, sir, of the sentiments of modern Christianity. You illustrate the deepest feelings in the heart of every man.]

[The LITTLE MAN rises with the BABY and a movement of approach.]

Guess I'm wanted in the dining-car.

[He vanishes. The LITTLE MAN sits down again, but back to the engine, away from the draught, and looks out of the window, patiently jogging the BABY On his knee.]

CURTAIN

SCENE III

An arrival platform. The LITTLE MAN, with the BABY and the
bundle, is standing disconsolate, while travellers pass and
luggage is being carried by. A STATION OFFICIAL, accompanied by
a POLICEMAN, appears from a doorway, behind him.

OFFICIAL. [Consulting telegram in his hand] 'Das ist der Herr'.

[They advance to the LITTLE MAN.]

OFFICIAL. 'Sie haben einen Buben gestohlen'?

LITTLE MAN. I only speak English and American.

OFFICIAL. 'Dies ist nicht Ihr Bube'?

[He touches the Baby.]

LITTLE MAN. [Shaking his head] Take care--it's ill.

[The man does not understand.]

Ill--the baby----

OFFICIAL. [Shaking his head] 'Verstehe nicht'. Dis is nod your baby?
No?

LITTLE MAN. [Shaking his head violently] No, it is not. No.

OFFICIAL. [Tapping the telegram] Gut! You are 'rested. [He signs
to the POLICEMAN, who takes the LITTLE MAN's arm.]

LITTLE MAN. Why? I don't want the poor baby.

OFFICIAL. [Lifting the bundle] 'Dies ist nicht Ihr Gepack'--pag?

LITTLE Mary. No.

OFFICIAL. Gut! You are 'rested.

LITTLE MAN. I only took it for the poor woman. I'm not a thief--I'm--I'm----

OFFICIAL. [Shaking head] Verstehe nicht.

  [The LITTLE MAN tries to tear his hair. The disturbed BABY
  wails.]

LITTLE MAN. [Dandling it as best he can] There, there--poor, poor!

OFFICIAL. Halt still! You are 'rested. It is all right.

LITTLE MAN. Where is the mother?

OFFICIAL. She comet by next drain. Das telegram say: 'Halt einen
Herren mit schwarzem Buben and schwarzem Gepack'. 'Rest gentleman
mit black baby and black--pag.

  [The LITTLE MAN turns up his eyes to heaven.]

OFFICIAL. 'Komm mit us'.

  [They take the LITTLE MAN toward the door from which they have
  come. A voice stops them.]

AMERICAN. [Speaking from as far away as may be] Just a moment!

[The OFFICIAL stops; the LITTLE MAN also stops and sits down on
a bench against the wall. The POLICEMAN stands stolidly beside
him. The AMERICAN approaches a step or two, beckoning; the
OFFICIAL goes up to him.]

AMERICAN. Guess you've got an angel from heaven there! What's the
gentleman in buttons for?

OFFICIAL. 'Was ist das'?

AMERICAN. Is there anybody here that can understand American?

OFFICIAL. 'Verstehe nicht'.

AMERICAN. Well, just watch my gestures. I was saying [He points to
the LITTLE MAN, then makes gestures of flying] you have an angel
from heaven there. You have there a man in whom Gawd [He points
upward] takes quite an amount of stock. You have no call to arrest
him. [He makes the gesture of arrest] No, Sir. Providence has
acted pretty mean, loading off that baby on him. [He makes the
motion of dandling] The little man has a heart of gold. [He points
to his heart, and takes out a gold coin.]

OFFICIAL. [Thinking he is about to be bribed] 'Aber, das ist zu
viel'!

AMERICAN. Now, don't rattle me! [Pointing to the LITTLE MAN] Man
[Pointing to his heart] 'Herz' [Pointing to the coin] 'von' Gold.
This is a flower of the field--he don't want no gentleman in buttons
to pluck him up.

[A little crowd is gathering, including the Two ENGLISH, the GERMAN, and the DUTCH YOUTH.]

OFFICIAL. 'Verstehe absolut nichts'. [He taps the telegram] 'Ich muss mein' duty do.

AMERICAN. But I'm telling you. This is a white man. This is probably the whitest man on Gawd's earth.

OFFICIAL. 'Das macht nichts'--gut or no gut, I muss mein duty do. [He turns to go toward the LITTLE MAN.]

AMERICAN. Oh! Very well, arrest him; do your duty. This baby has typhus.

[At the word "typhus" the OFFICIAL stops.]

AMERICAN. [Making gestures] First-class typhus, black typhus, schwarzen typhus. Now you have it. I'm kind o' sorry for you and the gentleman in buttons. Do your duty!

OFFICIAL. Typhus? Der Bub--die baby hat typhus?

AMERICAN. I'm telling you.

OFFICIAL. Gott im Himmel!

AMERICAN. [Spotting the GERMAN in the little throng] here's a gentleman will corroborate me.

OFFICIAL. [Much disturbed, and signing to the POLICEMAN to stand clear] Typhus! 'Aber das ist grasslich'!

AMERICAN. I kind o' thought you'd feel like that.

OFFICIAL. 'Die Sanitatsmachine! Gleich'!

[A PORTER goes to get it. From either side the broken half-moon of persons stand gazing at the LITTLE MAN, who sits unhappily dandling the BABY in the centre.]

OFFICIAL. [Raising his hands] 'Was zu thun'?

AMERICAN. Guess you'd better isolate the baby.

[A silence, during which the LITTLE MAN is heard faintly whistling and clucking to the BABY.]

OFFICIAL. [Referring once more to his telegram]

"'Rest gentleman mit black baby." [Shaking his head] Wir must de gentleman hold. [To the GERMAN] 'Bitte, mein Herr, sagen Sie ihm, den Buben zu niedersetzen'. [He makes the gesture of deposit.]

GERMAN. [To the LITTLE MAN] He say: Put down the baby.

[The LITTLE MAN shakes his head, and continues to dandle the BABY.]

OFFICIAL. You must.

[The LITTLE MAN glowers, in silence.]

ENGLISHMAN. [In background--muttering] Good man!

GERMAN. His spirit ever denies.

OFFICIAL. [Again making his gesture] 'Aber er muss'!

[The LITTLE MAN makes a face at him.]

'Sag' Ihm': Instantly put down baby, and komm' mit us.

[The BABY wails.]

LITTLE MAN. Leave the poor ill baby here alone? Be--be--be d---d to you!

AMERICAN. [Jumping on to a trunk--with enthusiasm] Bully!

[The ENGLISH clap their hands; the DUTCH YOUTH laughs. The OFFICIAL is muttering, greatly incensed.]

AMERICAN. What does that body-snatcher say?

GERMAN. He say this man use the baby to save himself from arrest. Very smart he say.

AMERICAN. I judge you do him an injustice. [Showing off the LITTLE MAN with a sweep of his arm.] This is a white man. He's got a black baby, and he won' leave it in the lurch. Guess we would all act noble that way, give us the chance.

[The LITTLE MAN rises, holding out the BABY, and advances a step or two. The half-moon at once gives, increasing its size; the AMERICAN climbs on to a higher trunk. The LITTLE MAN retires and again sits down.]

AMERICAN. [Addressing the OFFICIAL] Guess you'd better go out of business and wait for the mother.

OFFICIAL. [Stamping his foot] Die Mutter sall 'rested be for taking
out baby mit typhus. Ha! [To the LITTLE MAN] Put ze baby down!

   [The LITTLE MAN smiles.]

Do you 'ear?

AMERICAN. [Addressing the OFFICIAL] Now, see here. 'Pears to me
you don't suspicion just how beautiful this is. Here we have a man
giving his life for that old baby that's got no claim on him. This
is not a baby of his own making. No, sir, this is a very Christ-like
proposition in the gentleman.

OFFICIAL. Put ze baby down, or ich will goummand someone it to do.

AMERICAN. That will be very interesting to watch.

OFFICIAL. [To POLICEMAN] Dake it vrom him.

   [The POLICEMAN mutters, but does not.]

AMERICAN. [To the German] Guess I lost that.

GERMAN. He say he is not his officier.

AMERICAN. That just tickles me to death.

OFFICIAL. [Looking round] Vill nobody dake ze Bub'?

ENGLISHWOMAN. [Moving a step faintly] Yes--I----

ENGLISHMAN. [Grasping her arm]. By Jove! Will you!

OFFICIAL. [Gathering himself for a great effort to take the BABY, and advancing two steps] Zen I goummand you--[He stops and his voice dies away] Zit dere!

AMERICAN. My! That's wonderful. What a man this is! What a sublime sense of duty!

[The DUTCH YOUTH laughs. The OFFICIAL turns on him, but as he does so the MOTHER of the Busy is seen hurrying.]

MOTHER. 'Ach! Ach! Mei' Bubi'!

[Her face is illumined; she is about to rush to the LITTLE MAN.]

OFFICIAL. [To the POLICEMAN] 'Nimm die Frau'!

[The POLICEMAN catches hold of the WOMAN.]

OFFICIAL. [To the frightened WOMAN] 'Warum haben Sie einen Buben mit
'Typhus mit ausgebracht'?

AMERICAN. [Eagerly, from his perch] What was that? I don't want to miss any.

GERMAN. He say: Why did you a baby with typhus with you bring out?

AMERICAN. Well, that's quite a question.

[He takes out the field-glasses slung around him and adjusts them on the BABY.]

MOTHER. [Bewildered] Mei' Bubi--Typhus--aber Typhus? [She shakes her head violently] 'Nein, nein, nein! Typhus'!

OFFICIAL. Er hat Typhus.

MOTHER. [Shaking her head] 'Nein, nein, nein'!

AMERICAN. [Looking through his glasses] Guess she's kind of right! I judge the typhus is where the baby' slobbered on the shawl, and it's come off on him.

[The DUTCH YOUTH laughs.]

OFFICIAL. [Turning on him furiously] Er hat Typhus.

AMERICAN. Now, that's where you slop over. Come right here.

[The OFFICIAL mounts, and looks through the glasses.]

AMERICAN. [To the LITTLE MAN] Skin out the baby's leg. If we don't locate spots on that, it'll be good enough for me.

[The LITTLE MAN fumbles Out the BABY'S little white foot.]

MOTHER. Mei' Bubi! [She tries to break away.]

AMERICAN. White as a banana. [To the OFFICIAL--affably] Guess you've made kind of a fool of us with your old typhus.

OFFICIAL. Lass die Frau!

[The POLICEMAN lets her go, and she rushes to her BABY.]

MOTHER. Mei' Bubi!

[The BABY, exchanging the warmth of the LITTLE MAN for the momentary chill of its MOTHER, wails.]

OFFICIAL. [Descending and beckoning to the POLICEMAN] 'Sie wollen den Herrn accusiren'?

[The POLICEMAN takes the LITTLE MAN's arm.]

AMERICAN. What's that? They goin' to pitch him after all?

[The MOTHER, still hugging her BABY, who has stopped crying, gazes at the LITTLE MAN, who sits dazedly looking up. Suddenly she drops on her knees, and with her free hand lifts his booted foot and kisses it.]

AMERICAN. [Waving his hat] Ra! Ra! [He descends swiftly, goes up to the LITTLE MAN, whose arm the POLICEMAN has dropped, and takes his hand] Brother; I am proud to know you. This is one of the greatest moments I have ever experienced. [Displaying the LITTLE MAN to the assembled company] I think I sense the situation when I say that we all esteem it an honour to breathe the rather inferior atmosphere of this station here Along with our little friend. I guess we shall all go home and treasure the memory of his face as the whitest thing in our museum of recollections. And perhaps this good woman will also go home and wash the face of our little brother here. I am inspired with a new faith in mankind. Ladies and gentlemen, I wish to present to you a sure-enough saint--only wants a halo, to be transfigured. [To the LITTLE MAN] Stand right up.

[The LITTLE MAN stands up bewildered. They come about him. The OFFICIAL bows to him, the POLICEMAN salutes him. The DUTCH YOUTH shakes his head and laughs. The GERMAN draws himself up very straight, and bows quickly twice. The ENGLISHMAN and his

WIFE approach at least two steps, then, thinking better of it, turn to each other and recede. The MOTHER kisses his hand. The PORTER returning with the Sanitatsmachine, turns it on from behind, and its pinkish shower, goldened by a ray of sunlight, falls around the LITTLE MAN's head, transfiguring it as he stands with eyes upraised to see whence the portent comes.]

AMERICAN. [Rushing forward and dropping on his knees] Hold on just a minute! Guess I'll take a snapshot of the miracle. [He adjusts his pocket camera] This ought to look bully!

CURTAIN

FROM THE SERIES OF SIX SHORT PLAYS

HALL-MARKED

The scene is the sitting-room and verandah of HER bungalow.

The room is pleasant, and along the back, where the verandah runs, it seems all window, both French and casement. There is a door right and a door left. The day is bright; the time morning.

[HERSELF, dripping wet, comes running along the verandah, through the French window, with a wet Scotch terrier in her arms. She vanishes through the door left. A little pause, and LADY ELLA comes running, dry, thin, refined, and agitated. She halts where the tracks of water cease at the door left. A little pause, and MAUD comes running, fairly dry, stolid, breathless, and dragging a bull-dog, wet, breathless, and stout, by the crutch end of her 'en-tout-cas'].

LADY ELLA. Don't bring Hannibal in till I know where she's put Edward!

MAUD. [Brutally, to HANNIBAL] Bad dog! Bad dog!

[HANNIBAL snuffles.]

LADY ELLA. Maud, do take him out! Tie him up. Here! [She takes
out a lace handkerchief] No--something stronger! Poor darling
Edward! [To HANNIBAL] You are a bad dog!

[HANNIBAL snuffles.]

MAUD. Edward began it, Ella. [To HANNIBAL] Bad dog! Bad dog!

[HANNIBAL snuffles.]

LADY ELLA. Tie him up outside. Here, take my scarf. Where is my
poor treasure? [She removes her scarf] Catch! His ear's torn; I
saw it.

MAUD. [Taking the scarf, to HANNIBAL] Now!

[HANNIBAL snuffles.]

[She ties the scarf to his collar]

He smells horrible. Bad dog--getting into ponds to fight!

LADY ELLA. Tie him up, Maud. I must try in here.

[Their husbands, THE SQUIRE and THE RECTOR, come hastening along
the verandah.]

MAUD. [To THE RECTOR] Smell him, Bertie! [To THE SQUIRE] You
might have that pond drained, Squire!

[She takes HANNIBAL out, and ties him to the verandah. THE

SQUIRE and RECTOR Come in. LADY ELLA is knocking on the door left.]

HER VOICE. All right! I've bound him up!

LADY ELLA. May I come in?

HER VOICE. Just a second! I've got nothing on.

[LADY ELLA recoils. THE SQUIRE and RECTOR make an involuntary movement of approach.]

LADY ELLA. Oh! There you are!

THE RECTOR. [Doubtfully] I was just going to wade in----

LADY ELLA. Hannibal would have killed him, if she hadn't rushed in!

THE SQUIRE. Done him good, little beast!

LADY ELLA. Why didn't you go in, Tommy?

THE SQUIRE. Well, I would--only she----

LADY ELLA. I can't think how she got Edward out of Hannibal's awful mouth!

MAUD. [Without--to HANNIBAL, who is snuffling on the verandah and straining at the scarf] Bad dog!

LADY ELLA. We must simply thank her tremendously! I shall never forget the way she ran in, with her skirts up to her waist!

THE SQUIRE. By Jove! No. It was topping.

LADY ELLA. Her clothes must be ruined. That pond--ugh! [She wrinkles her nose] Tommy, do have it drained.

THE RECTOR. [Dreamily] I don't remember her face in church.

THE SQUIRE. Ah! Yes. Who is she? Pretty woman!

LADY ELLA. I must get the Vet. to Edward. [To THE SQUIRE] Tommy, do exert yourself!

  [MAUD re-enters.]

THE SQUIRE. All right! [Exerting himself] Here's a bell!

HER VOICE. [Through the door] The bleeding's stopped. Shall I send him in to you?

LADY ELLA. Oh, please! Poor darling!

  [They listen.]

  [LADY ELLA, prepares to receive EDWARD. THE SQUIRE and RECTOR stand transfixed. The door opens, and a bare arm gently pushes EDWARD forth. He is bandaged with a smooth towel. There is a snuffle--HANNIBAL has broken the scarf, outside.]

LADY ELLA. [Aghast] Look! Hannibal's loose! Maud--Tommy. [To THE RECTOR] You!

  [The THREE rush to prevent HANNIBAL from re-entering.]

LADY ELLA. [To EDWARD] Yes, I know--you'd like to! You SHALL bite him when it's safe. Oh! my darling, you DO----[She sniffs].

[MAUD and THE SQUIRE re-enter.]

Have you tied him properly this time?

MAUD. With Bertie's braces.

LADY ELLA. Oh! but----

MAUD. It's all right; they're almost leather.

[THE RECTOR re-enters, with a slight look of insecurity.]

LADY ELLA. Rector, are you sure it's safe?

THE RECTOR. [Hitching at his trousers] No, indeed, LADY Ella--I----

LADY ELLA. Tommy, do lend a hand!

THE SQUIRE. All right, Ella; all right! He doesn't mean what you mean!

LADY ELLA. [Transferring EDWARD to THE SQUIRE] Hold him, Tommy. He's sure to smell out Hannibal!

THE SQUIRE. [Taking EDWARD by the collar, and holding his own nose] Jove! Clever if he can smell anything but himself. Phew! She ought to have the Victoria Cross for goin' in that pond.

[The door opens, and HERSELF appears; a fine, frank, handsome woman, in a man's orange-coloured motor-coat, hastily thrown on over the substrata of costume.]

SHE. So very sorry--had to have a bath, and change, of course!

LADY ELLA. We're so awfully grateful to you. It was splendid.

MAUD. Quite.

THE RECTOR. [Rather holding himself together] Heroic! I was just myself about to----

THE SQUIRE. [Restraining EDWARD] Little beast will fight--must apologise--you were too quick for me----

[He looks up at her. She is smiling, and regarding the wounded dog, her head benevolently on one side.]

SHE. Poor dears! They thought they were so safe in that nice pond!

LADY ELLA. Is he very badly torn?

SHE. Rather nasty. There ought to be a stitch or two put in his ear.

LADY ELLA. I thought so. Tommy, do----

THE SQUIRE. All right. Am I to let him go?

LADY ELLA. No.

MAUD. The fly's outside. Bertie, run and tell Jarvis to drive in for the Vet.

THE RECTOR. [Gentle and embarrassed] Run? Well, Maud--I----

SHE. The doctor would sew it up. My maid can go round.

[HANNIBAL. appears at the open casement with the broken braces dangling from his collar.]

LADY ELLA. Look! Catch him! Rector!

MAUD. Bertie! Catch him!

[THE RECTOR seizes HANNIBAL, but is seen to be in difficulties with his garments. HERSELF, who has gone out left, returns, with a leather strop in one hand and a pair of braces in the other.]

SHE. Take this strop--he can't break that. And would these be any good to you?

[SHE hands the braces to MAUD and goes out on to the verandah and hastily away. MAUD, transferring the braces to the RECTOR, goes out, draws HANNIBAL from the casement window, and secures him with the strap. THE RECTOR sits suddenly with the braces in his hands. There is a moment's peace.]

LADY ELLA. Splendid, isn't she? I do admire her.

THE SQUIRE. She's all there.

THE RECTOR. [Feelingly] Most kind.

[He looks ruefully at the braces and at LADY ELLA. A silence. MAUD reappears at the door and stands gazing at the braces.]

THE SQUIRE. [Suddenly] Eh?

MAUD. Yes.

THE SQUIRE. [Looking at his wife] Ah!

LADY ELLA. [Absorbed in EDWARD] Poor darling!

THE SQUIRE. [Bluntly] Ella, the Rector wants to get up!

THE RECTOR. [Gently] Perhaps--just for a moment----

LADY ELLA. Oh! [She turns to the wall.]

[THE RECTOR, screened by his WIFE, retires on to the verandah to adjust his garments.]

THE SQUIRE. [Meditating] So she's married!

LADY ELLA. [Absorbed in EDWARD] Why?

THE SQUIRE. Braces.

LADY ELLA. Oh! Yes. We ought to ask them to dinner, Tommy.

THE SQUIRE. Ah! Yes. Wonder who they are?

[THE RECTOR and MAUD reappear.]

THE RECTOR. Really very good of her to lend her husband's--I was--er--quite----

MAUD. That'll do, Bertie.

[THEY see HER returning along the verandah, followed by a sandy, red-faced gentleman in leather leggings, with a needle and cotton in his hand.]

HERSELF. Caught the doctor just starting, So lucky!

LADY ELLA. Oh! Thank goodness!

DOCTOR. How do, Lady Ella? How do, Squire?--how do, Rector? [To MAUD] How de do? This the beastie? I see. Quite! Who'll hold him for me?

LADY ELLA. Oh! I!

HERSELF. D'you know, I think I'd better. It's so dreadful when it's your own, isn't it? Shall we go in here, doctor? Come along, pretty boy!

[She takes EDWARD, and they pass into the room, left.]

LADY ELLA. I dreaded it. She is splendid!

THE SQUIRE. Dogs take to her. That's a sure sign.

THE RECTOR. Little things--one can always tell.

THE SQUIRE. Something very attractive about her--what! Fine build of woman.

MAUD. I shall get hold of her for parish work.

THE RECTOR. Ah! Excellent--excellent! Do!

THE SQUIRE. Wonder if her husband shoots? She seems quite-er--quite----

LADY ELLA. [Watching the door] Quite! Altogether charming; one of the nicest faces I ever saw.

[THE DOCTOR comes out alone.]

Oh! Doctor--have you? is it----?

DOCTOR. Right as rain! She held him like an angel--he just licked her, and never made a sound.

LADY ELLA. Poor darling! Can I----

[She signs toward the door.]

DOCTOR. Better leave 'em a minute. She's moppin' 'im off. [He wrinkles his nose] Wonderful clever hands!

THE SQUIRE. I say--who is she?

DOCTOR. [Looking from face to face with a dubious and rather quizzical expression] Who? Well--there you have me! All I know is she's a first-rate nurse--been helpin' me with a case in Ditch Lane. Nice woman, too--thorough good sort! Quite an acquisition here. H'm! [Again that quizzical glance] Excuse me hurryin' off--very late. Good-bye, Rector. Good-bye, Lady Ella. Good-bye!

[He goes. A silence.]

THE SQUIRE. H'm! I suppose we ought to be a bit careful.

[JARVIS, flyman of the old school, has appeared on the verandah.]

JARVIS. [To THE RECTOR] Beg pardon, sir. Is the little dog all right?

MAUD. Yes.

JARVIS. [Touching his hat] Seein' you've missed your train, m'm, shall I wait, and take you 'ome again?

MAUD. No.

JARVIS. Cert'nly, m'm. [He touches his hat with a circular gesture, and is about to withdraw.]

LADY ELLA. Oh, Jarvis--what's the name of the people here?

JARVIS. Challenger's the name I've driven 'em in, my lady.

THE SQUIRE. Challenger? Sounds like a hound. What's he like?

JARVIS. [Scratching his head] Wears a soft 'at, sir.

THE SQUIRE. H'm! Ah!

JARVIS. Very nice gentleman, very nice lady. 'Elped me with my old mare when she 'ad the 'ighsteria last week--couldn't 'a' been kinder if they'd 'a' been angels from 'eaven. Wonderful fond o' dumb animals, the two of 'em. I don't pay no attention to gossip, meself.

MAUD. Gossip? What gossip?

JARVIS. [Backing] Did I make use of the word, m'm? You'll excuse me, I'm sure. There's always talk where there's newcomers. I takes people as I finds 'em.

THE RECTOR. Yes, yes, Jarvis--quite--quite right!

JARVIS. Yes, sir. I've--I've got a 'abit that way at my time o' life.

MAUD. [Sharply] How long have they been here, Jarvis?

JARVIS. Well---er--a matter of three weeks, m'm.

   [A slight involuntary stir.]

[Apologetic] Of course, in my profession I can't afford to take notice of whether there's the trifle of a ring between 'em, as the sayin' is. 'Tisn't 'ardly my business like.

   [A silence.]

LADY ELLA. [Suddenly] Er--thank you, Jarvis; you needn't wait.

JARVIS. No, m'lady. Your service, sir--service, m'm.

   [He goes. A silence.]

THE SQUIRE. [Drawing a little closer] Three weeks? I say--er-- wasn't there a book?

THE RECTOR. [Abstracted] Three weeks----I certainly haven't seen them in church.

MAUD. A trifle of a ring!

LADY ELLA. [Impulsively] Oh, bother! I'm sure she's all right. And if she isn't, I don't care. She's been much too splendid.

THE SQUIRE. Must think of the village. Didn't quite like the doctor's way of puttin' us off.

LADY ELLA. The poor darling owes his life to her.

THE SQUIRE. H'm! Dash it! Yes! Can't forget the way she ran into that stinkin' pond.

MAUD. Had she a wedding-ring on?

   [They look at each other, but no one knows.]

LADY ELLA. Well, I'm not going to be ungrateful.

THE SQUIRE. It'd be dashed awkward--mustn't take a false step, Ella.

THE RECTOR. And I've got his braces! [He puts his hand to his waist.]

MAUD. [Warningly] Bertie!

THE SQUIRE. That's all right, Rector--we're goin' to be perfectly polite, and--and--thank her, and all that.

LADY ELLA. We can see she's a good sort. What does it matter?

MAUD. My dear Ella! "What does it matter!" We've got to know.

THE RECTOR. We do want light.

THE SQUIRE. I'll ring the bell. [He rings.]

[They look at each other aghast.]

LADY ELLA. What did you ring for, Tommy?

THE SQUIRE. [Flabbergasted] God knows!

MAUD. Somebody'll come.

THE SQUIRE. Rector--you--you've got to----

MAUD. Yes, Bertie.

THE RECTOR. Dear me! But--er--what--er----How?

THE SQUIRE. [Deeply-to himself] The whole thing's damn delicate.

[The door right is opened and a MAID appears. She is a determined-looking female. They face her in silence.]

THE RECTOR. Er--er----your master is not in?

THE MAID. No. 'E's gone up to London.

THE RECTOR. Er----Mr Challenger, I think?

THE MAID. Yes.

THE RECTOR. Yes! Er----quite so

THE MAID. [Eyeing them] D'you want--Mrs Challenger?

THE RECTOR. Ah! Not precisely----

THE SQUIRE. [To him in a low, determined voice] Go on.

THE RECTOR. [Desperately] I asked because there was a--a--Mr.
Challenger I used to know in the 'nineties, and I thought--you
wouldn't happen to know how long they've been married? My friend
marr----

THE MAID. Three weeks.

THE RECTOR. Quite so--quite so! I shall hope it will turn out to
be----Er--thank you--Ha!

LADY ELLA. Our dog has been fighting with the Rector's, and Mrs
Challenger rescued him; she's bathing his ear. We're waiting to
thank her. You needn't----

THE MAID. [Eyeing them] No.

  [She turns and goes out.]

THE SQUIRE. Phew! What a gorgon! I say, Rector, did you really
know a Challenger in the 'nineties?

THE RECTOR. [Wiping his brow] No.

THE SQUIRE. Ha! Jolly good!

LADY ELLA. Well, you see!--it's all right.

THE RECTOR. Yes, indeed. A great relief!

LADY ELLA. [Moving to the door] I must go in now.

THE SQUIRE. Hold on! You goin' to ask 'em to--to--anything?

LADY ELLA. Yes.

MAUD. I shouldn't.

LADY ELLA. Why not? We all like the look of her.

THE RECTOR. I think we should punish ourselves for entertaining that uncharitable thought.

LADY ELLA. Yes. It's horrible not having the courage to take people as they are.

THE SQUIRE. As they are? H'm! How can you till you know?

LADY ELLA. Trust our instincts, of course.

THE SQUIRE. And supposing she'd turned out not married--eh!

LADY ELLA! She'd still be herself, wouldn't she?

MAUD. Ella!

THE SQUIRE. H'm! Don't know about that.

LADY ELLA. Of course she would, Tommy.

THE RECTOR. [His hand stealing to his waist] Well! It's a great weight off my----!

LADY ELLA. There's the poor darling snuffling. I must go in.

[She knocks on the door. It is opened, and EDWARD comes out briskly, with a neat little white pointed ear-cap on one ear.]

LADY ELLA. Precious!

[SHE HERSELF Comes out, now properly dressed in flax-blue linen.]

LADY ELLA. How perfectly sweet of you to make him that!

SHE. He's such a dear. And the other poor dog?

MAUD. Quite safe, thanks to your strop.

[HANNIBAL appears at the window, with the broken strop dangling. Following her gaze, they turn and see him.]

MAUD. Oh! There, he's broken it. Bertie!

SHE. Let me! [She seizes HANNIBAL.]

THE SQUIRE. We're really most tremendously obliged to you. Afraid we've been an awful nuisance.

SHE. Not a bit. I love dogs.

THE SQUIRE. Hope to make the acquaintance of Mr----of your husband.

LADY ELLA. [To EDWARD, who is straining]

[Gently, darling! Tommy, take him.]

[THE SQUIRE does so.]

MAUD. [Approaching HANNIBAL.] Is he behaving?

[She stops short, and her face suddenly shoots forward at HER hands that are holding HANNIBAL'S neck.]

SHE. Oh! yes--he's a love.

MAUD. [Regaining her upright position, and pursing her lips; in a peculiar voice] Bertie, take Hannibal.

THE RECTOR takes him.

LADY ELLA. [Producing a card] I can't be too grateful for all you've done for my poor darling. This is where we live. Do come-- and see----

[MAUD, whose eyes have never left those hands, tweaks LADY ELLA's dress.]

LADY ELLA. That is--I'm--I----

[HERSELF looks at LADY ELLA in surprise.]

THE SQUIRE. I don't know if your husband shoots, but if----

[MAUD, catching his eye, taps the third finger of her left hand.]

--er--he--does--er--er----

[HERSELF looks at THE SQUIRE surprised.]

MAUD. [Turning to her husband, repeats the gesture with the low and simple word] Look!

THE RECTOR. [With round eyes, severely] Hannibal! [He lifts him bodily and carries him away.]

MAUD. Don't squeeze him, Bertie!

[She follows through the French window.]

THE SQUIRE. [Abruptly--of the unoffending EDWARD] That dog'll be forgettin' himself in a minute.

[He picks up EDWARD and takes him out.]

[LADY ELLA is left staring.]

LADY ELLA. [At last] You mustn't think, I----You mustn't think, we ----Oh! I must just see they--don't let Edward get at Hannibal.

[She skims away.]

[HERSELF is left staring after LADY ELLA, in surprise.]

SHE. What is the matter with them?

[The door is opened.]

THE MAID. [Entering and holding out a wedding-ring--severely] You left this, m'm, in the bathroom.

SHE. [Looking, startled, at her finger] Oh! [Taking it] I hadn't missed it. Thank you, Martha.

[THE MAID goes.]

[A hand, slipping in at the casement window, softly lays a pair of braces on the windowsill. SHE looks at the braces, then at the ring. HER lip curls.]

Sue. [Murmuring deeply] Ah!

CURTAIN

DEFEAT

A TINY DRAMA

CHARACTERS

THE OFFICER.
THE GIRL.

During the Great War. Evening.

An empty room. The curtains drawn and gas turned low. The furniture and walls give a colour-impression as of greens and beetroot. There is a prevalence of plush. A fireplace on the Left, a sofa, a small table; the curtained window is at the back. On the table, in a common pot, stands a little plant of maidenhair fern, fresh and green.

Enter from the door on the Right, a GIRL and a YOUNG OFFICER in khaki. The GIRL wears a discreet dark dress, hat, and veil, and stained yellow gloves. The YOUNG OFFICER is tall, with a fresh open face, and kindly eager blue eyes; he is a little lame. The

GIRL, who is evidently at home, moves towards the gas jet to
turn it up, then changes her mind, and going to the curtains,
draws them apart and throws up the window. Bright moonlight
comes flooding in. Outside are seen the trees of a little
Square. She stands gazing out, suddenly turns inward with a
shiver.

YOUNG OFF. I say; what's the matter? You were crying when I spoke
to you.

GIRL. [With a movement of recovery] Oh! nothing. The beautiful
evening-that's all.

YOUNG OFF. [Looking at her] Cheer up!

GIRL. [Taking of hat and veil; her hair is yellowish and crinkly]
Cheer up! You are not lonelee, like me.

YOUNG OFF. [Limping to the window--doubtfully] I say, how did you
how did you get into this? Isn't it an awfully hopeless sort of
life?

GIRL. Yees, it ees. You haf been wounded?

YOUNG OFF. Just out of hospital to-day.

GIRL. The horrible war--all the misery is because of the war. When
will it end?

YOUNG OFF. [Leaning against the window-sill, looking at her
attentively] I say, what nationality are you?

GIRL. [With a quick look and away] Rooshian.

YOUNG OFF. Really! I never met a Russian girl. [The GIRL gives him another quick look] I say, is it as bad as they make out?

GIRL. [Slipping her hand through his arm] Not when I haf anyone as ni-ice as you; I never haf had, though. [She smiles, and her smile, like her speech, is slow and confining] You stopped because I was sad, others stop because I am gay. I am not fond of men at all. When you know--you are not fond of them.

YOUNG OFF. Well, you hardly know them at their best, do you? You should see them in the trenches. By George! They're simply splendid--officers and men, every blessed soul. There's never been anything like it--just one long bit of jolly fine self-sacrifice; it's perfectly amazing.

GIRL. [Turning her blue-grey eyes on him] I expect you are not the last at that. You see in them what you haf in yourself, I think.

YOUNG OFF. Oh, not a bit; you're quite out! I assure you when we made the attack where I got wounded there wasn't a single man in my regiment who wasn't an absolute hero. The way they went in--never thinking of themselves--it was simply ripping.

GIRL. [In a queer voice] It is the same too, perhaps, with--the enemy.

YOUNG OFF. Oh, yes! I know that.

GIRL. Ah! You are not a mean man. How I hate mean men!

YOUNG OFF. Oh! they're not mean really--they simply don't understand.

GIRL. Oh! You are a babee--a good babee aren't you?

[The YOUNG OFFICER doesn't like this, and frowns. The GIRL looks a little scared.]

GIRL. [Clingingly] But I li-ke you for it. It is so good to find a ni-ice man.

YOUNG OFF. [Abruptly] About being lonely? Haven't you any Russian friends?

GIRL. [Blankly] Rooshian? No. [Quickly] The town is so beeg. Were you at the concert before you spoke to me?

YOUNG OFF. Yes.

GIRL. I too. I lofe music.

YOUNG OFF. I suppose all Russians do.

GIRL. [With another quick look tat him] I go there always when I haf the money.

YOUNG OFF. What! Are you as badly on the rocks as that?

GIRL. Well, I haf just one shilling now!

[She laughs bitterly. The laugh upsets him; he sits on the window-sill, and leans forward towards her.]

YOUNG OFF. I say, what's your name?

GIRL. May. Well, I call myself that. It is no good asking yours.

YOUNG OFF. [With a laugh] You're a distrustful little soul; aren't you?

GIRL. I haf reason to be, don't you think?

YOUNG OFF. Yes. I suppose you're bound to think us all brutes.

GIRL. [Sitting on a chair close to the window where the moonlight falls on one powdered cheek] Well, I haf a lot of reasons to be afraid all my time. I am dreadfully nervous now; I am not trusding anybody. I suppose you haf been killing lots of Germans?

YOUNG OFF. We never know, unless it happens to be hand to hand; I haven't come in for that yet.

GIRL. But you would be very glad if you had killed some.

YOUNG OFF. Oh, glad? I don't think so. We're all in the same boat, so far as that's concerned. We're not glad to kill each other--not most of us. We do our job--that's all.

GIRL. Oh! It is frightful. I expect I haf my brothers killed.

YOUNG OFF. Don't you get any news ever?

GIRL. News? No indeed, no news of anybody in my country. I might not haf a country; all that I ever knew is gone; fader, moder, sisters, broders, all; never any more I shall see them, I suppose, now. The war it breaks and breaks, it breaks hearts. [She gives a little snarl] Do you know what I was thinking when you came up to me? I was thinking of my native town, and the river in the moonlight. If I could see it again I would be glad. Were you ever homeseeck?

YOUNG OFF. Yes, I have been--in the trenches. But one's ashamed with all the others.

GIRL. Ah! Yees! Yees! You are all comrades there. What is it like for me here, do you think, where everybody hates and despises me, and would catch me and put me in prison, perhaps. [Her breast heaves.]

YOUNG OFF. [Leaning forward and patting her knee] Sorry--sorry.

GIRL. [In a smothered voice] You are the first who has been kind to me for so long! I will tell you the truth--I am not Rooshian at all --I am German.

YOUNG OFF. [Staring] My dear girl, who cares. We aren't fighting against women.

GIRL. [Peering at him] Another man said that to me. But he was thinkin' of his fun. You are a veree ni-ice boy; I am so glad I met you. You see the good in people, don't you? That is the first thing in the world--because--there is really not much good in people, you know.

YOUNG OFF. [Smiling] You are a dreadful little cynic! But of course you are!

GIRL. Cyneec? How long do you think I would live if I was not a cyneec? I should drown myself to-morrow. Perhaps there are good people, but, you see, I don't know them.

YOUNG OFF. I know lots.

GIRL. [Leaning towards him] Well now--see, ni-ice boy--you haf never been in a hole, haf you?

YOUNG OFF. I suppose not a real hole.

GIRL. No, I should think not, with your face. Well, suppose I am
still a good girl, as I was once, you know; and you took me to your
mother and your sisters and you said: "Here is a little German girl
that has no work, and no money, and no friends." They will say: "Oh!
how sad! A German girl!" And they will go and wash their hands.

[The OFFICER, is silent, staring at her.]

GIRL. You see.

YOUNG OFF. [Muttering] I'm sure there are people.

GIRL. No. They would not take a German, even if she was good.
Besides, I don't want to be good any more--I am not a humbug; I have
learned to be bad. Aren't you going to kees me, ni-ice boy?

She puts her face close to his. Her eyes trouble him; he draws back.

YOUNG OFF. Don't. I'd rather not, if you don't mind. [She looks at
him fixedly, with a curious inquiring stare] It's stupid. I don't
know--but you see, out there, and in hospital, life's different.
It's--it's--it isn't mean, you know. Don't come too close.

GIRL. Oh! You are fun----[She stops] Eesn't it light. No Zeps
to-night. When they burn--what a 'orrble death! And all the people
cheer. It is natural. Do you hate us veree much?

YOUNG OFF. [Turning sharply] Hate? I don't know.

GIRL. I don't hate even the English--I despise them. I despise my people too; even more, because they began this war. Oh! I know that. I despise all the peoples. Why haf they made the world so miserable --why haf they killed all our lives--hundreds and thousands and millions of lives--all for noting? They haf made a bad world-- everybody hating, and looking for the worst everywhere. They haf made me bad, I know. I believe no more in anything. What is there to believe in? Is there a God? No! Once I was teaching little English children their prayers--isn't that funnee? I was reading to them about Christ and love. I believed all those things. Now I believe noting at all--no one who is not a fool or a liar can believe. I would like to work in a 'ospital; I would like to go and 'elp poor boys like you. Because I am a German they would throw me out a 'undred times, even if I was good. It is the same in Germany, in France, in Russia, everywhere. But do you think I will believe in Love and Christ and God and all that--Not I! I think we are animals --that's all! Oh, yes! you fancy it is because my life has spoiled me. It is not that at all--that is not the worst thing in life. The men I take are not ni-ice, like you, but it's their nature; and--they help me to live, which is something for me, anyway. No, it is the men who think themselves great and good and make the war with their talk and their hate, killing us all--killing all the boys like you, and keeping poor People in prison, and telling us to go on hating; and all these dreadful cold-blood creatures who write in the papers --the same in my country--just the same; it is because of all of them that I think we are only animals.

[The YOUNG OFFICER gets up, acutely miserable.]

[She follows him with her eyes.]

GIRL. Don't mind me talkin', ni-ice boy. I don't know anyone to talk to. If you don't like it, I can be quiet as a mouse.

YOUNG OFF. Oh, go on! Talk away; I'm not obliged to believe you, and I don't.

[She, too, is on her feet now, leaning against the wall; her dark dress and white face just touched by the slanting moonlight. Her voice comes again, slow and soft and bitter.]

GIRL. Well, look here, ni-ice boy, what sort of world is it, where millions are being tortured, for no fault of theirs, at all? A beautiful world, isn't it? 'Umbog! Silly rot, as you boys call it. You say it is all "Comrades" and braveness out there at the front, and people don't think of themselves. Well, I don't think of myself veree much. What does it matter? I am lost now, anyway. But I think of my people at 'ome; how they suffer and grieve. I think of all the poor people there, and here, how lose those they love, and all the poor prisoners. Am I not to think of them? And if I do, how am I to believe it a beautiful world, ni-ice boy?

[He stands very still, staring at her.]

GIRL. Look here! We haf one life each, and soon it is over. Well, I think that is lucky.

YOUNG OFF. No! There's more than that.

GIRL. [Softly] Ah! You think the war is fought for the future; you are giving your lives for a better world, aren't you?

YOUNG OFF. We must fight till we win.

GIRL. Till you win. My people think that too. All the peoples think that if they win the world will be better. But it will not, you know; it will be much worse, anyway.

[He turns away from her, and catches up his cap. Her voice follows him.]

GIRL. I don't care which win. I don't care if my country is beaten. I despise them all--animals--animals. Ah! Don't go, ni-ice boy; I will be quiet now.

[He has taken some notes from his tunic pocket; he puts then on the table and goes up to her.]

YOUNG OFF. Good-night.

GIRL. [Plaintively] Are you really going? Don't you like me enough?

YOUNG OFF. Yes, I like you.

GIRL. It is because I am German, then?

YOUNG OFF. No.

GIRL. Then why won't you stay?

YOUNG OFF. [With a shrug] If you must know--because you upset me.

GIRL. Won't you kees me once?

[He bends, puts his lips to her forehead. But as he takes them away she throws her head back, presses her mouth to his, and clings to him.]

YOUNG OFF. [Sitting down suddenly] Don't! I don't want to feel a brute.

GIRL. [Laughing] You are a funny boy; but you are veree good. Talk to me a little, then. No one talks to me. Tell me, haf you seen many German prisoners?

YOUNG OFF. [Sighing] A good many.

GIRL. Any from the Rhine?

YOUNG OFF. Yes, I think so.

GIRL. Were they veree sad?

YOUNG OFF. Some were; some were quite glad to be taken.

GIRL. Did you ever see the Rhine? It will be wonderful to-night. The moonlight will be the same there, and in Rooshia too, and France, everywhere; and the trees will look the same as here, and people will meet under them and make love just as here. Oh! isn't it stupid, the war? As if it were not good to be alive!

YOUNG OFF. You can't tell how good it is to be alive till you're facing death. You don't live till then. And when a whole lot of you feel like that--and are ready to give their lives for each other, it's worth all the rest of life put together.

[He stops, ashamed of such, sentiment before this girl, who believes in nothing.]

GIRL. [Softly] How were you wounded, ni-ice boy?

YOUNG OFF. Attacking across open ground: four machine bullets got me at one go off.

GIRL. Weren't you veree frightened when they ordered you to attack?

[He shakes his head and laughs.]

YOUNG OFF. It was great. We did laugh that morning. They got me much too soon, though--a swindle.

GIRL. [Staring at him] You laughed?

YOUNG OFF. Yes. And what do you think was the first thing I was conscious of next morning? My old Colonel bending over me and giving me a squeeze of lemon. If you knew my Colonel you'd still believe in things. There is something, you know, behind all this evil. After all, you can only die once, and, if it's for your country--all the better!

[Her face, in the moonlight, with, intent eyes touched up with black, has a most strange, other-world look.]

GIRL. No; I believe in nothing, not even in my country. My heart is dead.

YOUNG OFF. Yes; you think so, but it isn't, you know, or you wouldn't have 'been crying when I met you.

GIRL. If it were not dead, do you think I could live my life-walking the streets every night, pretending to like strange men; never hearing a kind word; never talking, for fear I will be known for a German? Soon I shall take to drinking; then I shall be "Kaput" veree quick. You see, I am practical; I see things clear. To-night I am a little emotional; the moon is funny, you know. But I live for myself only, now. I don't care for anything or anybody.

YOUNG OFF. All the same; just now you were pitying your folk at home, and prisoners and that.

GIRL. Yees; because they suffer. Those who suffer are like me--I pity myself, that's all; I am different from your English women. I see what I am doing; I do not let my mind become a turnip just because I am no longer moral.

YOUNG OFF. Nor your heart either, for all you say.

GIRL. Ni-ice boy, you are veree obstinate. But all that about love is 'umbog. We love ourselves, noting more.

> At that intense soft bitterness in her voice, he gets up, feeling stifled, and stands at the window. A newspaper boy some way off is calling his wares. The GIRL's fingers slip between his own, and stay unmoving. He looks round into her face. In spite of make-up it has a queer, unholy, touching beauty.

YOUNG OFF. [With an outburst] No; we don't only love ourselves; there is more. I can't explain, but there's something great; there's kindness--and--and-----

[The shouting of newspaper boys grows louder and their cries, passionately vehement, clash into each other and obscure each word. His head goes up to listen; her hand tightens within his arm--she too is listening. The cries come nearer, hoarser, more shrill and clamorous; the empty moonlight outside seems suddenly crowded with figures, footsteps, voices, and a fierce distant cheering. "Great victory--great victory! Official! British! 'Eavy defeat of the 'Uns! Many thousand prisoners! 'Eavy defeat!" It speeds by, intoxicating, filling him with a fearful joy; he leans far out, waving his cap and cheering like a

madman; the night seems to flutter and vibrate and answer. He
turns to rush down into the street, strikes against something
soft, and recoils. The GIRL stands with hands clenched, and
face convulsed, panting. All confused with the desire to do
something, he stoops to kiss her hand. She snatches away her
fingers, sweeps up the notes he has put down, and holds them out
to him.]

GIRL. Take them--I will not haf your English money--take them.

Suddenly she tears them across, twice, thrice, lets the bits.
flutter to the floor, and turns her back on him. He stands
looking at her leaning against the plush-covered table, her head
down, a dark figure in a dark room, with the moonlight
sharpening her outline. Hardly a moment he stays, then makes
for the door. When he is gone, she still stands there, her chin
on her breast, with the sound in her ears of cheering, of
hurrying feet, and voices crying: "'Eavy Defeat!" stands, in the
centre of a pattern made by the fragments of the torn-up notes,
staring out unto the moonlight, seeing not this hated room and
the hated Square outside, but a German orchard, and herself, a
little girl, plucking apples, a big dog beside her; and a
hundred other pictures, such as the drowning see. Then she
sinks down on the floor, lays her forehead on the dusty carpet,
and presses her body to it. Mechanically, she sweeps together
the scattered fragments of notes, assembling them with the dust
into a little pile, as of fallen leaves, and dabbling in it with
her fingers, while the tears run down her cheeks.

GIRL. Defeat! Der Vaterland! Defeat! . . . One shillin'!

[Then suddenly, in the moonlight, she sits up, and begins to
sing with all her might "Die Wacht am Rhein." And outside men

pass, singing: "Rule, Britannia!"]

CURTAIN

THE SUN

A SCENE

CHARACTERS

THE GIRL.
THE MAN.
THE SOLDIER.

    A Girl, sits crouched over her knees on a stile close to a
river. A MAN with a silver badge stands beside her, clutching
the worn top plank. THE GIRL'S level brows are drawn together;
her eyes see her memories. THE MAN's eyes see THE GIRL; he has
a dark, twisted face. The bright sun shines; the quiet river
flows; the Cuckoo is calling; the mayflower is in bloom along
the hedge that ends in the stile on the towing-path.

THE GIRL. God knows what 'e'll say, Jim.

THE MAN. Let 'im. 'E's come too late, that's all.

THE GIRL. He couldn't come before. I'm frightened. 'E was fond o' me.

THE MAN. And aren't I fond of you?

THE GIRL. I ought to 'a waited, Jim; with 'im in the fightin'.

THE MAN. [Passionately] And what about me? Aren't I been in the fightin'--earned all I could get?

THE GIRL. [Touching him] Ah!

THE MAN. Did you--? [He cannot speak the words.]

THE GIRL. Not like you, Jim--not like you.

THE MAN. Have a spirit, then.

THE GIRL. I promised him.

THE MAN. One man's luck's another's poison.

THE GIRL. I ought to 'a waited. I never thought he'd come back from the fightin'.

THE MAN. [Grimly] Maybe 'e'd better not 'ave.

THE GIRL. [Looking back along the tow-path] What'll he be like, I wonder?

THE MAN. [Gripping her shoulder] Daisy, don't you never go back on me, or I should kill you, and 'im too.

[THE GIRL looks at him, shivers, and puts her lips to his.]

THE GIRL. I never could.

THE MAN. Will you run for it? 'E'd never find us!

[THE GIRL shakes her head.]

THE MAN [Dully] What's the good o' stayin'? The world's wide.

THE GIRL. I'd rather have it off me mind, with him home.

THE MAN. [Clenching his hands] It's temptin' Providence.

THE GIRL. What's the time, Jim?

THE MAN. [Glancing at the sun] 'Alf past four.

THE GIRL. [Looking along the towing-path] He said four o'clock. Jim, you better go.

THE MAN. Not I. I've not got the wind up. I've seen as much of hell as he has, any day. What like is he?

THE GIRL. [Dully] I dunno, just. I've not seen him these three years. I dunno no more, since I've known you.

THE MAN. Big or little chap?

THE GIRL. 'Bout your size. Oh! Jim, go along!

THE MAN. No fear! What's a blighter like that to old Fritz's shells? We didn't shift when they was comin'. If you'll go, I'll go; not else.

[Again she shakes her head.]

THE GIRL. Jim, do you love me true?

[For answer THE MAN takes her avidly in his arms.]

I ain't ashamed--I ain't ashamed. If 'e could see me 'eart.

THE MAN. Daisy! If I'd known you out there, I never could 'a stuck it. They'd 'a got me for a deserter. That's how I love you!

THE GIRL. Jim, don't lift your hand to 'im! Promise!

THE MAN. That's according.

THE GIRL. Promise!

THE MAN. If 'e keeps quiet, I won't. But I'm not accountable--not always, I tell you straight--not since I've been through that.

THE GIRL. [With a shiver] Nor p'raps he isn't.

THE MAN. Like as not. It takes the lynch pins out, I tell you.

THE GIRL. God 'elp us!

THE MAN. [Grimly] Ah! We said that a bit too often. What we want we take, now; there's no one else to give it us, and there's no fear'll stop us; we seen the bottom of things.

THE GIRL. P'raps he'll say that too.

THE MAN. Then it'll be 'im or me.

THE GIRL. I'm frightened:

THE MAN. [Tenderly] No, Daisy, no! The river's handy. One more or less. 'E shan't 'arm you; nor me neither. [He takes out a knife.]

THE GIRL. [Seizing his hand] Oh, no! Give it to me, Jim!

THE MAN. [Smiling] No fear! [He puts it away] Shan't 'ave no need for it like as not. All right, little Daisy; you can't be expected to see things like what we do. What's life, anyway? I've seen a thousand lives taken in five minutes. I've seen dead men on the wires like flies on a flypaper. I've been as good as dead meself a hundred times. I've killed a dozen men. It's nothin'. He's safe, if 'e don't get my blood up. If he does, nobody's safe; not 'im, nor anybody else; not even you. I'm speakin' sober.

THE GIRL. [Softly] Jim, you won't go fightin' in the sun, with the birds all callin'?

THE MAN. That depends on 'im. I'm not lookin' for it. Daisy, I love you. I love your hair. I love your eyes. I love you.

THE GIRL. And I love you, Jim. I don't want nothin' more than you in all the world.

THE MAN. Amen to that, my dear. Kiss me close!

> The sound of a voice singing breaks in on their embrace. THE GIRL starts from his arms, and looks behind her along the towing-path. THE MAN draws back against, the hedge, fingering his side, where the knife is hidden. The song comes nearer.

"I'll be right there to-night,
    Where the fields are snowy white;
    Banjos ringing, darkies singing,
    All the world seems bright."

THE GIRL. It's him!

THE MAN. Don't get the wind up, Daisy. I'm here!

[The singing stops. A man's voice says "Christ! It's Daisy;
it's little Daisy 'erself!" THE GIRL stands rigid. The figure
of a soldier appears on the other side of the stile. His cap is
tucked into his belt, his hair is bright in the sunshine; he is
lean, wasted, brown, and laughing.]

SOLDIER. Daisy! Daisy! Hallo, old pretty girl!

[THE GIRL does not move, barring the way, as it were.]

THE GIRL. Hallo, Jack! [Softly] I got things to tell you!

SOLDIER. What sort o' things, this lovely day? Why, I got things
that'd take me years to tell. Have you missed me, Daisy?

THE GIRL. You been so long.

SOLDIER. So I 'ave. My Gawd! It's a way they 'ave in the Army. I
said when I got out of it I'd laugh. Like as the sun itself I used
to think of you, Daisy, when the trumps was comin' over, and the wind
was up. D'you remember that last night in the wood? "Come back and
marry me quick, Jack." Well, here I am--got me pass to heaven. No
more fightin', no more drillin', no more sleepin' rough. We can get
married now, Daisy. We can live soft an' 'appy. Give us a kiss, my

dear.

THE GIRL. [Drawing back] No.

SOLDIER. [Blankly] Why not?

[THE MAN, with a swift movement steps along the hedge to THE GIRL'S side.]

THE MAN. That's why, soldier.

SOLDIER. [Leaping over the stile] 'Oo are you, Pompey? The sun don't shine in your inside, do it? 'Oo is he, Daisy?

THE GIRL. My man.

SOLDIER. Your-man! Lummy! "Taffy was a Welshman, Taffy was a thief!" Well, mate! So you've been through it, too. I'm laughin' this mornin' as luck will 'ave it. Ah! I can see your knife.

THE MAN. [Who has half drawn his knife] Don't laugh at me, I tell you.

SOLDIER. Not at you, not at you. [He looks from one to the other] I'm laughin' at things in general. Where did you get it, mate?

THE MAN. [Watchfully] Through the lung.

SOLDIER. Think o' that! An' I never was touched. Four years an' never was touched. An' so you've come an' took my girl! Nothin' doin'! Ha! [Again he looks from one to the other-then away] Well! The world's before me! [He laughs] I'll give you Daisy for a lung protector.

THE MAN. [Fiercely] You won't. I've took her.

SOLDIER. That's all right, then. You keep 'er. I've got a laugh in me you can't put out, black as you look! Good-bye, little Daisy!

[THE GIRL makes a movement towards him.]

THE MAN. Don't touch 'im!

[THE GIRL stands hesitating, and suddenly bursts into tears.]

SOLDIER. Look 'ere, mate; shake 'ands! I don't want to see a girl cry, this day of all, with the sun shinin'. I seen too much of sorrer. You and me've been at the back of it. We've 'ad our whack. Shake!

THE MAN. Who are you kiddin'? You never loved 'er!

SOLDIER. [After a long moment's pause] Oh! I thought I did.

THE MAN. I'll fight you for her.

[He drops his knife.]

SOLDIER. [Slowly] Mate, you done your bit, an' I done mine. It's took us two ways, seemin'ly.

THE GIRL. [Pleading] Jim!

THE MAN. [With clenched fists] I don't want 'is charity. I only want what I can take.

SOLDIER. Daisy, which of us will you 'ave?

THE GIRL. [Covering her face] Oh! Him!

SOLDIER. You see, mate! Put your 'ands down. There's nothin' for it but a laugh. You an' me know that. Laugh, mate!

THE MAN. You blarsted----!

[THE GIRL springs to him and stops his mouth.]

SOLDIER. It's no use, mate. I can't do it. I said I'd laugh to-day, and laugh I will. I've come through that, an' all the stink of it; I've come through sorrer. Never again! Cheerio, mate! The sun's a-shinin'! He turns away.

THE GIRL. Jack, don't think too 'ard of me!

SOLDIER. [Looking back] No fear, my dear! Enjoy your fancy! So long! Gawd bless you both!

He sings, and goes along the path, and the song fades away.

> "I'll be right there to-night
> Where the fields are snowy white;
> Banjos ringing, darkies singing
> All the world seems bright!"

THE MAN. 'E's mad!

THE GIRL. [Looking down the path with her hands clasped] The sun has touched 'im, Jim!

CURTAIN

PUNCH AND GO

A LITTLE COMEDY

"Orpheus with his lute made trees
And the mountain tope that freeze....."

PERSONS OF THE PLAY

JAMES G. FRUST ....The Boss
E. BLEWITT VANE ....The Producer
MR. FORESON ....The Stage Manager
"ELECTRICS"..................The Electrician
"PROPS" ....The Property Man
HERBERT ....The Call Boy

OF THE PLAY WITHIN THE PLAY

GUY TOONE ....The Professor
VANESSA HELLGROVE ....The Wife

GEORGE FLEETWAY ....Orpheus
MAUDE HOPKINS ....The Faun

SCENE: The Stage of a Theatre.

Action continuous, though the curtain is momentarily lowered according to that action.

The Scene is the stage of the theatre set for the dress rehearsal of the little play: "Orpheus with his Lute." The curtain is up and the audience, though present, is not supposed to be. The set scene represents the end section of a room, with wide French windows, Back Centre, fully opened on to an apple orchard in bloom. The Back Wall with these French windows, is set only about ten feet from the footlights, and the rest of the stage is orchard. What is visible of the room would indicate the study of a writing man of culture. (Note.--If found advantageous for scenic purposes, this section of room can be changed to a broad verandah or porch with pillars supporting its roof.) In the wall, Stage Left, is a curtained opening, across which the curtain is half drawn. Stage Right of the French windows is a large armchair turned rather towards the window, with a book rest attached, on which is a volume of the Encyclopedia Britannica, while on a stool alongside are writing materials such as a man requires when he writes with a pad on his knees. On a little table close by is a reading-lamp with a dark green shade. A crude light from the floats makes the stage stare; the only person on it is MR FORESON, the stage manager, who is standing in the centre looking upwards as if waiting for someone to speak. He is a short, broad man, rather blank, and fatal. From the back of the auditorium, or from an empty box, whichever is most convenient, the producer, MR BLEWITT VANE, a man of about thirty four, with his hair brushed back, speaks.

VANE. Mr Foreson?

FORESON. Sir?

VANE. We'll do that lighting again.

[FORESON walks straight of the Stage into the wings Right.]

[A pause.]

Mr Foreson! [Crescendo] Mr Foreson.

[FORESON walks on again from Right and shades his eyes.]

VANE. For goodness sake, stand by! We'll do that lighting again. Check your floats.

FORESON. [Speaking up into the prompt wings] Electrics!

VOICE OF ELECTRICS. Hallo!

FORESON. Give it us again. Check your floats.

[The floats go down, and there is a sudden blinding glare of blue lights, in which FORESON looks particularly ghastly.]

VANE. Great Scott! What the blazes! Mr Foreson!

[FORESON walks straight out into the wings Left. Crescendo.]

Mr Foreson!

FORESON. [Re-appearing] Sir?

VANE. Tell Miller to come down.

FORESON. Electrics! Mr Blewitt Vane wants to speak to you. Come down!

VANE. Tell Herbert to sit in that chair.

[FORESON walks straight out into the Right wings.]

Mr Foreson!

FORESON. [Re-appearing] Sir?

VANE. Don't go off the stage. [FORESON mutters.]

[ELECTRICS appears from the wings, Stage Left. He is a dark, thin-faced man with rather spikey hair.]

ELECTRICS. Yes, Mr Vane?

VANE. Look!

ELECTRICS. That's what I'd got marked, Mr Vane.

VANE. Once for all, what I want is the orchard in full moonlight, and the room dark except for the reading lamp. Cut off your front battens.

[ELECTRICS withdraws Left. FORESON walks off the Stage into the Right wings.]

Mr Foreson!

FORESON. [Re-appearing] Sir?

VANE. See this marked right. Now, come on with it! I want to get some beauty into this!

[While he is speaking, HERBERT, the call boy, appears from the wings Right, a mercurial youth of about sixteen with a wide mouth.]

FORESON. [Maliciously] Here you are, then, Mr Vane. Herbert, sit in that chair.

[HERBERT sits an the armchair, with an air of perfect peace.]

VANE. Now! [All the lights go out. In a wail] Great Scott!

[A throaty chuckle from FORESON in the darkness. The light dances up, flickers, shifts, grows steady, falling on the orchard outside. The reading lamp darts alight and a piercing little glare from it strikes into the auditorium away from HERBERT.]

[In a terrible voice] Mr Foreson.

FORESON. Sir?

VANE. Look--at--that--shade!

[FORESON mutters, walks up to it and turns it round so that the light shines on HERBERT'S legs.]

On his face, on his face!

[FORESON turns the light accordingly.]

FORESON. Is that what you want, Mr Vane?

VANE. Yes. Now, mark that!

FORESON. [Up into wings Right] Electrics!

ELECTRICS. Hallo!

FORESON. Mark that!

VANE. My God!

[The blue suddenly becomes amber.]

[The blue returns. All is steady. HERBERT is seen diverting himself with an imaginary cigar.]

Mr Foreson.

FORESON. Sir?

VANE. Ask him if he's got that?

FORESON. Have you got that?

ELECTRICS. Yes.

VANE. Now pass to the change. Take your floats off altogether.

FORESON. [Calling up] Floats out. [They go out.]

VANE. Cut off that lamp. [The lamp goes out] Put a little amber in your back batten. Mark that! Now pass to the end. Mr Foreson!

FORESON. Sir?

VANE. Black out

FORESON. [Calling up] Black out!

[The lights go out.]

VANE. Give us your first lighting-lamp on. And then the two changes. Quick as you can. Put some pep into it. Mr Foreson!

FORESON. Sir?

VANE. Stand for me where Miss Hellgrove comes in. FORESON crosses to the window. No, no!--by the curtain.

[FORESON takes his stand by the curtain; and suddenly the three lighting effects are rendered quickly and with miraculous exactness.]

Good! Leave it at that. We'll begin. Mr Foreson, send up to Mr Frust.

[He moves from the auditorium and ascends on to the Stage, by some steps Stage Right.]

FORESON. Herb! Call the boss, and tell beginners to stand by. Sharp, now!

[HERBERT gets out of the chair, and goes off Right.]

[FORESON is going off Left as VANE mounts the Stage.]

VANE. Mr Foreson.

FORESON. [Re-appearing] Sir?

VANE. I want "Props."

FORESON. [In a stentorian voice] "Props!"

[Another moth-eaten man appears through the French windows.]

VANE. Is that boulder firm?

PROPS. [Going to where, in front of the back-cloth, and apparently among its apple trees, lies the counterfeitment of a mossy boulder; he puts his foot on it] If, you don't put too much weight on it, sir.

VANE. It won't creak?

PROPS. Nao. [He mounts on it, and a dolorous creaking arises.]

VANE. Make that right. Let me see that lute.

[PROPS produces a property lute. While they scrutinize it, a broad man with broad leathery clean-shaven face and small mouth, occupied by the butt end of a cigar, has come on to the stage from Stage Left, and stands waiting to be noticed.]

PROPS. [Attracted by the scent of the cigar] The Boss, Sir.

VANE. [Turning to "PROPS"] That'll do, then.

["PROPS" goes out through the French windows.]

VANE. [To FRUST] Now, sir, we're all ready for rehearsal of "Orpheus with his Lute."

FRUST. [In a cosmopolitan voice] "Orphoos with his loot!" That his loot, Mr Vane? Why didn't he pinch something more precious? Has this high-brow curtain-raiser of yours got any "pep" in it?

VANE. It has charm.

FRUST. I'd thought of "Pop goes the Weasel" with little Miggs. We kind of want a cock-tail before "Louisa loses," Mr Vane.

VANE. Well, sir, you'll see.

FRUST. This your lighting? It's a bit on the spiritool side. I've left my glass. Guess I'll sit in the front row. Ha'f a minute. Who plays this Orphoos?

VANE. George Fleetway.

FRUST. Has he got punch?

VANE. It's a very small part.

FRUST. Who are the others?

VANE. Guy Toone plays the Professor; Vanessa Hellgrove his wife; Maude Hopkins the faun.

FRUST. H'm! Names don't draw.

VANE. They're not expensive, any of them. Miss Hellgrove's a find, I think.

FRUST. Pretty?

VANE. Quite.

FRUST. Arty?

VANE. [Doubtfully] No. [With resolution] Look here, Mr FRUST, it's no use your expecting another "Pop goes the Weasel."

FRUST. We-ell, if it's got punch and go, that'll be enough for me. Let's get to it!

> [He extinguishes his cigar and descends the steps and sits in the centre of the front row of the stalls.]

VANE. Mr Foreson?

FORESON. [Appearing through curtain, Right] Sir?

VANE. Beginners. Take your curtain down.

> [He descends the steps and seats himself next to FRUST. The curtain goes down.]

> [A woman's voice is heard singing very beautifully Sullivan's

song: "Orpheus with his lute, with his lute made trees and the mountain tops that freeze'." etc.]

FRUST. Some voice!

The curtain rises. In the armchair the PROFESSOR is yawning, tall, thin, abstracted, and slightly grizzled in the hair. He has a pad of paper over his knee, ink on the stool to his right and the Encyclopedia volume on the stand to his left-barricaded in fact by the article he is writing. He is reading a page over to himself, but the words are drowned in the sound of the song his WIFE is singing in the next room, partly screened off by the curtain. She finishes, and stops. His voice can then be heard conning the words of his article.

PROF. "Orpheus symbolized the voice of Beauty, the call of life, luring us mortals with his song back from the graves we dig for ourselves. Probably the ancients realized this neither more nor less than we moderns. Mankind has not changed. The civilized being still hides the faun and the dryad within its broadcloth and its silk. And yet"--[He stops, with a dried-up air-rather impatiently] Go on, my dear! It helps the atmosphere.

[The voice of his WIFE begins again, gets as far as "made them sing" and stops dead, just as the PROFESSOR's pen is beginning to scratch. And suddenly, drawing the curtain further aside]

[SHE appears. Much younger than the PROFESSOR, pale, very pretty, of a Botticellian type in face, figure, and in her clinging cream-coloured frock. She gazes at her abstracted husband; then swiftly moves to the lintel of the open window, and stands looking out.]

THE WIFE. God! What beauty!

PROF. [Looking Up] Umm?

THE WIFE. I said: God! What beauty!

PROF. Aha!

THE WIFE. [Looking at him] Do you know that I have to repeat everything to you nowadays?

PROF. What?

THE WIFE. That I have to repeat----

PROF. Yes; I heard. I'm sorry. I get absorbed.

THE WIFE. In all but me.

PROF. [Startled] My dear, your song was helping me like anything to get the mood. This paper is the very deuce--to balance between the historical and the natural.

THE WIFE. Who wants the natural?

PROF. [Grumbling] Umm! Wish I thought that! Modern taste! History may go hang; they're all for tuppence-coloured sentiment nowadays.

THE WIFE. [As if to herself] Is the Spring sentiment?

PROF. I beg your pardon, my dear; I didn't catch.

WIFE. [As if against her will--urged by some pent-up force] Beauty, beauty!

PROF. That's what I'm trying to say here. The Orpheus legend symbolizes to this day the call of Beauty! [He takes up his pen, while she continues to stare out at the moonlight. Yawning] Dash it! I get so sleepy; I wish you'd tell them to make the after-dinner coffee twice as strong.

WIFE. I will.

PROF. How does this strike you? [Conning] "Many Renaissance pictures, especially those of Botticelli, Francesca and Piero di Cosimo were inspired by such legends as that of Orpheus, and we owe a tiny gem--like Raphael 'Apollo and Marsyas' to the same Pagan inspiration."

WIFE. We owe it more than that--rebellion against the dry-as-dust.

PROF. Quite. I might develop that: "We owe it our revolt against the academic; or our disgust at 'big business,' and all the grossness of commercial success. We owe----". [His voice peters out.]

WIFE. It--love.

PROF. [Abstracted] Eh!

WIFE. I said: We owe it love.

PROF. [Rather startled] Possibly. But--er [With a dry smile] I mustn't say that here--hardly!

WIFE. [To herself and the moonlight] Orpheus with his lute!

PROF. Most people think a lute is a sort of flute. [Yawning heavily] My dear, if you're not going to sing again, d'you mind sitting down? I want to concentrate.

WIFE. I'm going out.

PROF. Mind the dew!

WIFE. The Christian virtues and the dew.

PROF. [With a little dry laugh] Not bad! Not bad! The Christian virtues and the dew. [His hand takes up his pen, his face droops over his paper, while his wife looks at him with a very strange face] "How far we can trace the modern resurgence against the Christian virtues to the symbolic figures of Orpheus, Pan, Apollo, and Bacchus might be difficult to estimate, but----"

   [During those words his WIFE has passed through the window into the moonlight, and her voice rises, singing as she goes: "Orpheus with his lute, with his lute made trees . . ."]

PROF. [Suddenly aware of something] She'll get her throat bad. [He is silent as the voice swells in the distance] Sounds queer at night-H'm! [He is silent--Yawning. The voice dies away. Suddenly his head nods; he fights his drowsiness; writes a word or two, nods again, and in twenty seconds is asleep.]

   [The Stage is darkened by a black-out. FRUST's voice is heard speaking.]

FRUST. What's that girl's name?

VANE. Vanessa Hellgrove.

FRUST. Aha!

[The Stage is lighted up again. Moonlight bright on the orchard; the room in darkness where the PROFESSOR'S figure is just visible sleeping in the chair, and screwed a little more round towards the window. From behind the mossy boulder a faun-like figure uncurls itself and peeps over with ears standing up and elbows leaning on the stone, playing a rustic pipe; and there are seen two rabbits and a fox sitting up and listening. A shiver of wind passes, blowing petals from the apple-trees.]

[The FAUN darts his head towards where, from Right, comes slowly the figure of a Greek youth, holding a lute or lyre which his fingers strike, lifting out little wandering strains as of wind whinnying in funnels and odd corners. The FAUN darts down behind the stone, and the youth stands by the boulder playing his lute. Slowly while he plays the whitened trunk of an apple-tree is seen, to dissolve into the body of a girl with bare arms and feet, her dark hair unbound, and the face of the PROFESSOR'S WIFE. Hypnotized, she slowly sways towards him, their eyes fixed on each other, till she is quite close. Her arms go out to him, cling round his neck and, their lips meet. But as they meet there comes a gasp and the PROFESSOR with rumpled hair is seen starting from his chair, his hands thrown up; and at his horrified "Oh!" the Stage is darkened with a black-out.]

[The voice of FRUST is heard speaking.]

FRUST. Gee!

The Stage is lighted up again, as in the opening scene. The

PROFESSOR is seen in his chair, with spilt sheets of paper round him, waking from a dream. He shakes himself, pinches his leg, stares heavily round into the moonlight, rises.

PROF. Phew! Beastly dream! Boof! H'm! [He moves to the window and calls.] Blanche! Blanche! [To himself] Made trees-made trees! [Calling] Blanche!

WIFE's VOICE. Yes.

PROF. Where are you?

WIFE. [Appearing by the stone with her hair down] Here!

PROF. I say--I---I've been asleep--had a dream. Come in. I'll tell you.

[She comes, and they stand in the window.]

PROF. I dreamed I saw a-faun on that boulder blowing on a pipe. [He looks nervously at the stone] With two damned little rabbits and a fox sitting up and listening. And then from out there came our friend Orpheus playing on his confounded lute, till he actually turned that tree there into you. And gradually he-he drew you like a snake till you--er--put your arms round his neck and--er--kissed him. Boof! I woke up. Most unpleasant. Why! Your hair's down!

WIFE. Yes.

PROF. Why?

WIFE. It was no dream. He was bringing me to life.

PROF. What on earth?

WIFE. Do you suppose I am alive? I'm as dead as Euridice.

PROF. Good heavens, Blanche, what's the matter with you to-night?

WIFE. [Pointing to the litter of papers] Why don't we live, instead of writing of it? [She points out unto the moonlight] What do we get out of life? Money, fame, fashion, talk, learning? Yes. And what good are they? I want to live!

PROF. [Helplessly] My dear, I really don't know what you mean.

WIFE. [Pointing out into the moonlight] Look! Orpheus with his lute, and nobody can see him. Beauty, beauty, beauty--we let it go. [With sudden passion] Beauty, love, the spring. They should be in us, and they're all outside.

PROF. My dear, this is--this is--awful. [He tries to embrace her.]

WIFE. [Avoiding him--an a stilly voice] Oh! Go on with your writing!

PROF. I'm--I'm upset. I've never known you so--so----

WIFE. Hysterical? Well! It's over. I'll go and sing.

PROF. [Soothingly] There, there! I'm sorry, darling; I really am. You're kipped--you're kipped. [He gives and she accepts a kiss] Better?

[He gravitates towards his papers.]

All right, now?

WIFE. [Standing still and looking at him] Quite!

PROF. Well, I'll try and finish this to-night; then, to-morrow we might have a jaunt. How about a theatre? There's a thing--they say --called "Chinese Chops," that's been running years.

WIFE. [Softly to herself as he settles down into his chair] Oh! God!

[While he takes up a sheet of paper and adjusts himself, she stands at the window staring with all her might at the boulder, till from behind it the faun's head and shoulders emerge once more.]

PROF. Very queer the power suggestion has over the mind. Very queer! There's nothing really in animism, you know, except the curious shapes rocks, trees and things take in certain lights--effect they have on our imagination. [He looks up] What's the matter now?

WIFE. [Startled] Nothing! Nothing!

[Her eyes waver to him again, and the FAUN vanishes. She turns again to look at the boulder; there is nothing there; a little shiver of wind blows some petals off the trees. She catches one of them, and turning quickly, goes out through the curtain.]

PROF. [Coming to himself and writing] "The Orpheus legend is the-- er--apotheosis of animism. Can we accept----" [His voice is lost in the sound of his WIFE'S voice beginning again: "Orpheus with his lute--with his lute made trees----" It dies in a sob. The PROFESSOR looks up startled, as the curtain falls].

FRUST. Fine! Fine!

VANE. Take up the curtain. Mr Foreson?

  [The curtain goes up.]

FORESON. Sir?

VANE. Everybody on.

  [He and FRUST leave their seats and ascend on to the Stage, on
  which are collecting the four Players.]

VANE. Give us some light.

FORESON. Electrics! Turn up your floats!

  [The footlights go up, and the blue goes out; the light is crude
  as at the beginning.]

FRUST. I'd like to meet Miss Hellgrove. [She comes forward eagerly
and timidly. He grasps her hand] Miss Hellgrove, I want to say I
thought that fine--fine. [Her evident emotion and pleasure warm him
so that he increases his grasp and commendation] Fine. It quite got
my soft spots. Emotional. Fine!

MISS H. Oh! Mr Frust; it means so much to me. Thank you!

FRUST. [A little balder in the eye, and losing warmth] Er--fine!
[His eye wanders] Where's Mr Flatway?

VANE. Fleetway.

[FLEETWAY comes up.]

FRUST. Mr Fleetway, I want to say I thought your Orphoos very remarkable. Fine.

FLEETWAY. Thank you, sir, indeed--so glad you liked it.

FRUST. [A little balder in the eye] There wasn't much to it, but what there was was fine. Mr Toone.

[FLEETWAY melts out and TOONE is precipitated.]

Mr Toone, I was very pleased with your Professor--quite a character-study. [TOONE bows and murmurs] Yes, sir! I thought it fine. [His eye grows bald] Who plays the goat?

MISS HOPK. [Appearing suddenly between the windows] I play the faun, Mr Frost.

FORESON. [Introducing] Miss Maude 'Opkins.

FRUST. Miss Hopkins, I guess your fawn was fine.

MISS HOPK. Oh! Thank you, Mr Frost. How nice of you to say so. I do so enjoy playing him.

FRUST. [His eye growing bald] Mr Foreson, I thought the way you fixed that tree was very cunning; I certainly did. Got a match?

[He takes a match from FORESON, and lighting a very long cigar, walks up Stage through the French windows followed by FORESON, and examines the apple-tree.]

[The two Actors depart, but Miss HELLGROVE runs from where she has been lingering, by the curtain, to VANE, Stage Right.]

MISS H. Oh! Mr Vane--do you think? He seemed quite--Oh! Mr Vane [ecstatically] If only----

VANE. [Pleased and happy] Yes, yes. All right--you were splendid. He liked it. He quite----

MISS H. [Clasping her hand] How wonderful Oh, Mr Vane, thank you!

[She clasps his hands; but suddenly, seeing that FRUST is coming back, fits across into the curtain and vanishes.]

[The Stage, in the crude light, as empty now save for FRUST, who, in the French windows, Centre, is mumbling his cigar; and VANE, Stage Right, who is looking up into the wings, Stage Left.]

VANE. [Calling up] That lighting's just right now, Miller. Got it marked carefully?

ELECTRICS. Yes, Mr Vane.

VANE. Good. [To FRUST who as coming down] Well, sir? So glad----

FRUST. Mr Vane, we got little Miggs on contract?

VANE. Yes.

FRUST. Well, I liked that little pocket piece fine. But I'm blamed if I know what it's all about.

VANE. [A little staggered] Why! Of course it's a little allegory. The tragedy of civilization--all real feeling for Beauty and Nature kept out, or pent up even in the cultured.

FRUST. Ye-ep. [Meditatively] Little Miggs'd be fine in "Pop goes the Weasel."

VANE. Yes, he'd be all right, but----

FRUST. Get him on the 'phone, and put it into rehearsal right now.

VANE. What! But this piece--I--I----!

FRUST. Guess we can't take liberties with our public, Mr Vane. They want pep.

VANE. [Distressed] But it'll break that girl's heart. I--really--I can't----

FRUST. Give her the part of the 'tweeny in "Pop goes".

VANE. Mr Frust, I--I beg. I've taken a lot of trouble with this little play. It's good. It's that girl's chance--and I----

FRUST. We-ell! I certainly thought she was fine. Now, you 'phone up Miggs, and get right along with it. I've only one rule, sir! Give the Public what it wants; and what the Public wants is punch and go. They've got no use for Beauty, Allegory, all that high-brow racket. I know 'em as I know my hand.

[During this speech MISS HELLGROVE is seen listening by the French window, in distress, unnoticed by either of them.]

VANE. Mr Frost, the Public would take this, I'm sure they would; I'm convinced of it. You underrate them.

FRUST. Now, see here, Mr Blewitt Vane, is this my theatre? I tell you, I can't afford luxuries.

VANE. But it--it moved you, sir; I saw it. I was watching.

FRUST. [With unmoved finality] Mr Vane, I judge I'm not the average man. Before "Louisa Loses" the Public'll want a stimulant. "Pop goes the Weasel" will suit us fine. So--get right along with it. I'll go get some lunch.

   [As he vanishes into the wings, Left, MISS HELLGROVE covers her face with her hands. A little sob escaping her attracts VANE'S attention. He takes a step towards her, but she flies.]

VANE. [Dashing his hands through his hair till it stands up] Damnation!

   [FORESON walks on from the wings, Right.]

FORESON. Sir?

VANE. "Punch and go!" That superstition!

   [FORESON walks straight out into the wings, Left.]

VANE. Mr Foreson!

FORESON. [Re-appearing] Sir?

VANE. This is scrapped. [With savagery] Tell 'em to set the first act of "Louisa Loses," and put some pep into it.

[He goes out through the French windows with the wind still in his hair.]

FORESON. [In the centre of the Stage] Electrics!

ELECTRICS. Hallo!

FORESON. Where's Charlie?

ELECTRICS. Gone to his dinner.

FORESON. Anybody on the curtain?

A VOICE. Yes, Mr Foreson.

FORESON. Put your curtain down.

[He stands in the centre of the Stage with eyes uplifted as the curtain descends.]

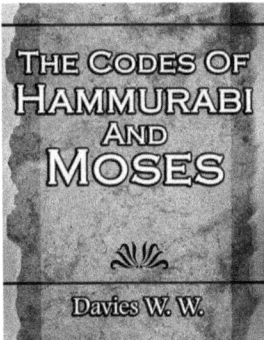

The Codes Of Hammurabi And Moses
W. W. Davies

QTY

The discovery of the Hammurabi Code is one of the greatest achievements of archaeology, and is of paramount interest, not only to the student of the Bible, but also to all those interested in ancient history...

Religion   ISBN: *1-59462-338-4*   **Pages:132**
MSRP $12.95

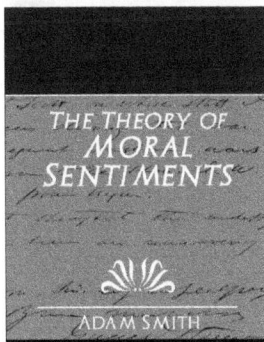

The Theory of Moral Sentiments
Adam Smith

QTY

This work from 1749. contains original theories of conscience amd moral judgment and it is the foundation for systemof morals.

Philosophy ISBN: *1-59462-777-0*   **Pages:536**
MSRP $19.95

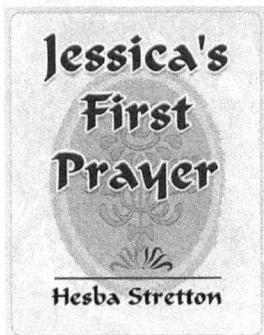

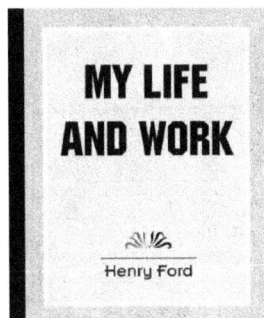

Jessica's First Prayer
Hesba Stretton

QTY

In a screened and secluded corner of one of the many railway-bridges which span the streets of London there could be seen a few years ago, from five o'clock every morning until half past eight, a tidily set-out coffee-stall, consisting of a trestle and board, upon which stood two large tin cans, with a small fire of charcoal burning under each so as to keep the coffee boiling during the early hours of the morning when the work-people were thronging into the city on their way to their daily toil...

Pages:84

Childrens   ISBN: *1-59462-373-2*   *MSRP $9.95*

My Life and Work
Henry Ford

QTY

Henry Ford revolutionized the world with his implementation of mass production for the Model T automobile. Gain valuable business insight into his life and work with his own auto-biography... "We have only started on our development of our country we have not as yet, with all our talk of wonderful progress, done more than scratch the surface. The progress has been wonderful enough but..."

Pages:300

Biographies/   ISBN: *1-59462-198-5*   *MSRP $21.95*

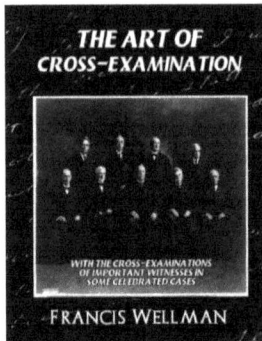

The Art of Cross-Examination
Francis Wellman

QTY

I presume it is the experience of every author, after his first book is published upon an important subject, to be almost overwhelmed with a wealth of ideas and illustrations which could readily have been included in his book, and which to his own mind, at least, seem to make a second edition inevitable. Such certainly was the case with me; and when the first edition had reached its sixth impression in five months, I rejoiced to learn that it seemed to my publishers that the book had met with a sufficiently favorable reception to justify a second and considerably enlarged edition. ..

Pages:412

Reference   ISBN: *1-59462-647-2*   *MSRP $19.95*

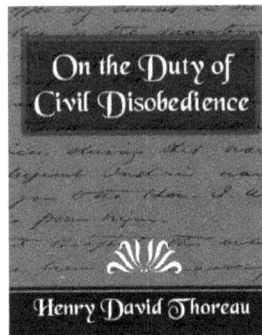

On the Duty of Civil Disobedience
Henry David Thoreau

QTY

Thoreau wrote his famous essay, On the Duty of Civil Disobedience, as a protest against an unjust but popular war and the immoral but popular institution of slave-owning. He did more than write—he declined to pay his taxes, and was hauled off to gaol in consequence. Who can say how much this refusal of his hastened the end of the war and of slavery ?

Law   ISBN: *1-59462-747-9*   **Pages:48**
                                          MSRP $7.45

Dream Psychology Psychoanalysis for Beginners
Sigmund Freud

QTY

Sigmund Freud, born Sigismund Schlomo Freud (May 6, 1856 - September 23, 1939), was a Jewish-Austrian neurologist and psychiatrist who co-founded the psychoanalytic school of psychology. Freud is best known for his theories of the unconscious mind, especially involving the mechanism of repression; his redefinition of sexual desire as mobile and directed towards a wide variety of objects; and his therapeutic techniques, especially his understanding of transference in the therapeutic relationship and the presumed value of dreams as sources of insight into unconscious desires.

Pages:196

Psychology   ISBN: *1-59462-905-6*   *MSRP $15.45*

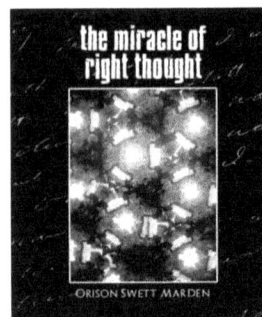

The Miracle of Right Thought
Orison Swett Marden

QTY

Believe with all of your heart that you will do what you were made to do. When the mind has once formed the habit of holding cheerful, happy, prosperous pictures, it will not be easy to form the opposite habit. It does not matter how improbable or how far away this realization may see, or how dark the prospects may be, if we visualize them as best we can, as vividly as possible, hold tenaciously to them and vigorously struggle to attain them, they will gradually become actualized, realized in the life. But a desire, a longing without endeavor, a yearning abandoned or held indifferently will vanish without realization.

Pages:360

Self Help   ISBN: *1-59462-644-8*   *MSRP $25.45*

The Rosicrucian Cosmo-Conception Mystic Christianity *by Max Heindel*   ISBN: *1-59462-188-8*   **$38.95**
The Rosicrucian Cosmo-conception is not dogmatic, neither does it appeal to any other authority than the reason of the student. It is: not controversial, but is: sent forth in the, hope that it may help to clear...   New Age/Religion Pages 646

Abandonment To Divine Providence *by Jean-Pierre de Caussade*   ISBN: *1-59462-228-0*   **$25.95**
"The Rev. Jean Pierre de Caussade was one of the most remarkable spiritual writers of the Society of Jesus in France in the 18th Century. His death took place at Toulouse in 1751. His works have gone through many editions and have been republished...   Inspirational/Religion Pages 400

Mental Chemistry *by Charles Haanel*   ISBN: *1-59462-192-6*   **$23.95**
Mental Chemistry allows the change of material conditions by combining and appropriately utilizing the power of the mind. Much like applied chemistry creates something new and unique out of careful combinations of chemicals the mastery of mental chemistry...   New Age Pages 354

The Letters of Robert Browning and Elizabeth Barret Barrett 1845-1846 vol II   ISBN: *1-59462-193-4*   **$35.95**
by Robert Browning and Elizabeth Barrett   Biographies Pages 596

Gleanings In Genesis (volume I) *by Arthur W. Pink*   ISBN: *1-59462-130-6*   **$27.45**
Appropriately has Genesis been termed "the seed plot of the Bible" for in it we have, in germ form, almost all of the great doctrines which are afterwards fully developed in the books of Scripture which follow...   Religion/Inspirational Pages 420

The Master Key *by L. W. de Laurence*   ISBN: *1-59462-001-6*   **$30.95**
In no branch of human knowledge has there been a more lively increase of the spirit of research during the past few years than in the study of Psychology, Concentration and Mental Discipline. The requests for authentic lessons in Thought Control, Mental Discipline and...   New Age/Business Pages 422

The Lesser Key Of Solomon Goetia *by L. W. de Laurence*   ISBN: *1-59462-092-X*   **$9.95**
This translation of the first book of the "Lernegton" which is now for the first time made accessible to students of Talismanic Magic was done, after careful collation and edition, from numerous Ancient Manuscripts in Hebrew, Latin, and French...   New Age/Occult Pages 92

Rubaiyat Of Omar Khayyam *by Edward Fitzgerald*   ISBN: *1-59462-332-5*   **$13.95**
Edward Fitzgerald, whom the world has already learned, in spite of his own efforts to remain within the shadow of anonymity, to look upon as one of the rarest poets of the century, was born at Bredfield, in Suffolk, on the 31st of March, 1809. He was the third son of John Purcell...   Music Pages 172

Ancient Law *by Henry Maine*   ISBN: *1-59462-128-4*   **$29.95**
The chief object of the following pages is to indicate some of the earliest ideas of mankind, as they are reflected in Ancient Law, and to point out the relation of those ideas to modern thought.   Religiom/History Pages 452

Far-Away Stories *by William J. Locke*   ISBN: *1-59462-129-2*   **$19.45**
"Good wine needs no bush, but a collection of mixed vintages does. And this book is just such a collection. Some of the stories I do not want to remain buried for ever in the museum files of dead magazine-numbers an author's not unpardonable vanity..."   Fiction Pages 272

Life of David Crockett *by David Crockett*   ISBN: *1-59462-250-7*   **$27.45**
"Colonel David Crockett was one of the most remarkable men of the times in which he lived. Born in humble life, but gifted with a strong will, an indomitable courage, and unremitting perseverance...   Biographies/New Age Pages 424

Lip-Reading *by Edward Nitchie*   ISBN: *1-59462-206-X*   **$25.95**
Edward B. Nitchie, founder of the New York School for the Hard of Hearing, now the Nitchie School of Lip-Reading, Inc, wrote "LIP-READING Principles and Practice". The development and perfecting of this meritorious work on lip-reading was an undertaking...   How-to Pages 400

A Handbook of Suggestive Therapeutics, Applied Hypnotism, Psychic Science   ISBN: *1-59462-214-0*   **$24.95**
by Henry Munro   Health/New Age/Health/Self-help Pages 376

A Doll's House: and Two Other Plays *by Henrik Ibsen*   ISBN: *1-59462-112-8*   **$19.95**
Henrik Ibsen created this classic when in revolutionary 1848 Rome. Introducing some striking concepts in playwriting for the realist genre, this play has been studied the world over.   Fiction/Classics/Plays 308

The Light of Asia *by sir Edwin Arnold*   ISBN: *1-59462-204-3*   **$13.95**
In this poetic masterpiece, Edwin Arnold describes the life and teachings of Buddha. The man who was to become known as Buddha to the world was born as Prince Gautama of India but he rejected the worldly riches and abandoned the reigns of power when...   Religion/History/Biographies Pages 170

The Complete Works of Guy de Maupassant *by Guy de Maupassant*   ISBN: *1-59462-157-8*   **$16.95**
"For days and days, nights and nights, I had dreamed of that first kiss which was to consecrate our engagement, and I knew not on what spot I should put my lips..."   Fiction/Classics Pages 240

The Art of Cross-Examination *by Francis L. Wellman*   ISBN: *1-59462-309-0*   **$26.95**
Written by a renowned trial lawyer, Wellman imparts his experience and uses case studies to explain how to use psychology to extract desired information through questioning.   How-to/Science/Reference Pages 408

Answered or Unanswered? *by Louisa Vaughan*   ISBN: *1-59462-248-5*   **$10.95**
Miracles of Faith in China   Religion Pages 112

The Edinburgh Lectures on Mental Science (1909) *by Thomas*   ISBN: *1-59462-008-3*   **$11.95**
This book contains the substance of a course of lectures recently given by the writer in the Queen Street Hail, Edinburgh. Its purpose is to indicate the Natural Principles governing the relation between Mental Action and Material Conditions...   New Age/Psychology Pages 148

Ayesha *by H. Rider Haggard*   ISBN: *1-59462-301-5*   **$24.95**
Verily and indeed it is the unexpected that happens! Probably if there was one person upon the earth from whom the Editor of this, and of a certain previous history, did not expect to hear again...   Classics Pages 380

Ayala's Angel *by Anthony Trollope*   ISBN: *1-59462-352-X*   **$29.95**
The two girls were both pretty, but Lucy who was twenty-one who supposed to be simple and comparatively unattractive, whereas Ayala was credited, as her Bombwhat romantic name might show, with poetic charm and a taste for romance. Ayala when her father died was nineteen...   Fiction Pages 484

The American Commonwealth *by James Bryce*   ISBN: *1-59462-286-8*   **$34.45**
An interpretation of American democratic political theory. It examines political mechanics and society from the perspective of Scotsman James Bryce   Politics Pages 572

Stories of the Pilgrims *by Margaret P. Pumphrey*   ISBN: *1-59462-116-0*   **$17.95**
This book explores pilgrims religious oppression in England as well as their escape to Holland and eventual crossing to America on the Mayflower, and their early days in New England...   History Pages 268

QTY

The Fasting Cure *by Sinclair Upton*   ISBN: *1-59462-222-1*   **$13.95**
In the Cosmopolitan Magazine for May, 1910, and in the Contemporary Review (London) for April, 1910, I published an article dealing with my experiences in fasting. I have written a great many magazine articles, but never one which attracted so much attention... New Age/Self Help/Health Pages 164

Hebrew Astrology *by Sepharial*   ISBN: *1-59462-308-2*   **$13.45**
In these days of advanced thinking it is a matter of common observation that we have left many of the old landmarks behind and that we are now pressing forward to greater heights and to a wider horizon than that which represented the mind-content of our progenitors...   Astrology Pages 144

Thought Vibration or The Law of Attraction in the Thought World   ISBN: *1-59462-127-6*   **$12.95**

by William Walker Atkinson   *Psychology/Religion Pages 144*

Optimism *by Helen Keller*   ISBN: *1-59462-108-X*   **$15.95**
Helen Keller was blind, deaf, and mute since 19 months old, yet famously learned how to overcome these handicaps, communicate with the world, and spread her lectures promoting optimism. An inspiring read for everyone...   Biographies/Inspirational Pages 84

Sara Crewe *by Frances Burnett*   ISBN: *1-59462-360-0*   **$9.45**
In the first place, Miss Minchin lived in London. Her home was a large, dull, tall one, in a large, dull square, where all the houses were alike, and all the sparrows were alike, and where all the door-knockers made the same heavy sound...   Childrens/Classic Pages 88

The Autobiography of Benjamin Franklin *by Benjamin Franklin*   ISBN: *1-59462-135-7*   **$24.95**
The Autobiography of Benjamin Franklin has probably been more extensively read than any other American historical work, and no other book of its kind has had such ups and downs of fortune. Franklin lived for many years in England, where he was agent...   Biographies/History Pages 332

Name	
Email	
Telephone	
Address	
City, State ZIP	

☐ **Credit Card**   ☐ **Check / Money Order**

Credit Card Number	
Expiration Date	
Signature	

Please Mail to: Book Jungle
PO Box 2226
Champaign, IL 61825
or Fax to: 630-214-0564

ORDERING INFORMATION

web: *www.bookjungle.com*
email: *sales@bookjungle.com*
fax: *630-214-0564*
mail: *Book Jungle PO Box 2226 Champaign, IL 61825*
or PayPal *to sales@bookjungle.com*

Please contact us for bulk discounts

DIRECT-ORDER TERMS

**20% Discount if You Order
Two or More Books**
Free Domestic Shipping!
Accepted: Master Card, Visa,
Discover, American Express

www.ingramcontent.com/pod-product-compliance
Lightning Source LLC
Chambersburg PA
CBHW050352100426
42739CB00015BB/3376